The Pygmalion Project:
Love and Coercion Among the Types

The Pygmalion Project:

Love and Coercion Among the Types

Stephen Montgomery

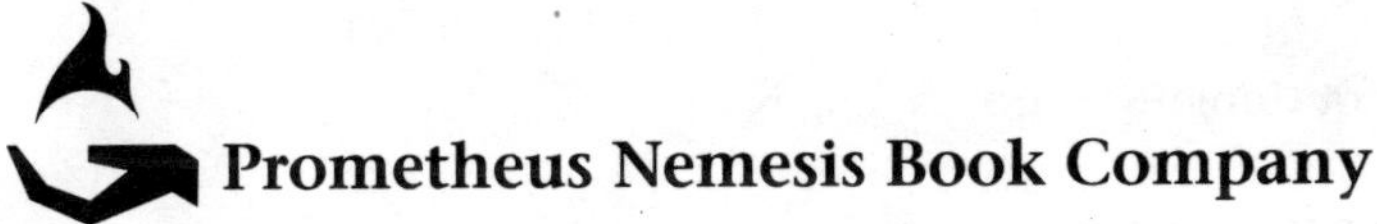

Cover and Interior Design: Gary Palmatier
Composition: Ideas to Images
Printing and Bindery: Delta Lithographers

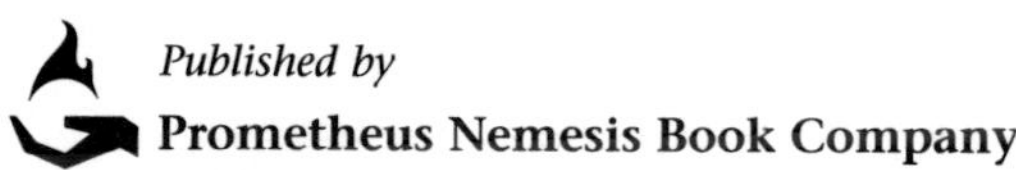

 Published in the United States by Prometheus Nemesis Book Company, Post Office Box 2748, Del Mar, CA 92014.

First Edition
Printed in the United States of America

10 9 8 7 6 5 4 3 2 1

Library of Congress Card Catalog No:

ISBN 0-9606954-2-7
$9.95

Volume One:

The Artisan

Acknowledgements

Thanks are due the following publishers for permission to reprint passages from the works indicated:

Curtis Brown Ltd.: *The Berlin Stories*, by Christopher Isherwood, copyright 1935; *The Horse's Mouth*, by Joyce Cary, copyright 1957, with permission of the trustees of the Joyce Cary Estate.

Samuel French, Inc.: *Hedda Gabler*, by Henrik Ibsen, trans. Rolf Fjelde, copyright 1965.

Houghton Mifflin Co.: *Vanity Fair,* by William Makepeace Thackeray, copyright 1963.

Grove Press, Inc.: *The Norman Conquests,* by Alan Ayckbourne, copyright 1975.

Alfred A. Knopf, Inc.: *The Stranger,* by Albert Camus, trans. Stuart Gilbert, copyright 1946.

Macmillan Publishing Co.: *A Farewell to Arms*, by Ernest Hemingway, copyright 1957; *The Great Gatsby*, by F. Scott Fitzgerald, copyright 1953; *In Our Time*, by Ernest Hemingway, copyright 1958; and *The Sun Also Rises*, by Ernest Hemingway, copyright 1970.

New Amercian Library: *Lady Chatterley's Lover,* by D. H. Lawrence, copyright 1959.

Viking Penguin, Inc.: *Sons and Lovers*, by D.H. Lawrence, copyright 1913.

Contents

Chapter 3

Chapter 4

Chapter 5

Foreword

Not often do we find someone with a perspective both broad enough and deep enough to span the enormous gap that lies between scientific and aesthetic fictions. Stephen Montgomery's many years as a teacher of literature, his doctoral studies in communication theory and literature, as well as his extensive experience with temperament theory (editing *Please Understand Me*), have made him perhaps uniquely qualified to unite the typologist's model of human relationships with the insights of the literary imagination.

This volume on the Pygmalion Project is indeed unique in its blending of temperament psychology, communication theory, and literary criticism. Most behavioral scientists have steadfastly disdained typology as a legitimate discipline, associating it with phrenology and astrology, neither of which is even remotely connected with it. At the same time, many communications analysts, failing to appreciate human differences, have argued that different styles of communication result from differences in *situation*, ignoring the simple fact that situations themselves differ with the temperament of those who create them. And, to my knowledge, no literary critic has attempted to analyze the manipulative communications—the games and strategies and tactics—of literary characters from the point of view of temperament theory.

Throughout his career, Dr. Montgomery has been deeply interested in the paradoxical communications that afflict human relationships. He has carefully studied those pioneering behavioral scientists—anthropologist Gregory Bateson, communications analyst Jay Haley, and that wizard from Phoenix, healer Milton Erickson—who have been most gifted in defining characterological communications in the "double binds" of human systems. And is not Montgomery's subject of the Pygmalion Project another classic paradoxical interacton? If in truth we seek to transform our loved ones into our own image, what happens if we succeed? If we were attracted in the first place by our loved ones' differences, can we be anything but dissatisfied by changing them into copies of ourselves? In other words, if we win the battle to change our loved ones, do we not actually lose in the relationship? And if we lose the battle, do we not actually win? This seems a paradox worthy of study, and in this book Montgomery ingeniously examines how the authors of a dozen aesthetic fictions describe the causes and the twisted effects of Pygmalion Projects in our most intimate relationships.

This first volume of Montgomery's proposed series focuses on the Artisan's special style of interpersonal coercion with Guardian, Idealist, and Rational loved ones, although we get hints throughout the book of how these other temperaments might go about sculpting their mates. Since the Artisans comprise as much as forty percent of the population—and since almost all of us have fallen for an Artisan at one time or another—it may be enlightening to learn about their inimitable style of loving, and how they seek to change us.

David Keirsey,
September 1988

Introduction: The Mirror of Fiction

> *It is not our purpose to become each other; it is to recognize each other, to learn to see the other and honor him for what he is.*
>
> —Hermann Hesse[1]

In Greek legend, Pygmalion, a brilliant young sculptor from Cyprus, was so disgusted (yet, strangely, so obsessed) with women's imperfections that he resolved to carve a statue of his ideal woman, embodying every feminine grace and virtue. Determined to perfect in his art what he found so flawed in flesh and blood, Pygmalion labored with all his skill and devotion, shaping here, smoothing there, until he had fashioned the most exquisite sculpture he could imagine. So exquisite indeed was his creation that Pygmalion fell passionately in love with the figure, and could be seen in his studio kissing its marble lips, fingering its marble hands, dressing and grooming the statue as if caring for a doll. Despite the work's perfection, however, Pygmalion was desperately unhappy, for the lifeless statue could not respond to his

---

[1] Hermann Hesse, *Narcissus and Goldmund*, p. 43.

desires, the cold stone could not return the warmth of his love. He had set out to shape his idea of the perfect woman, but had succeeded only in creating his own frustration and despair.[2]

The premise of this book is that, in many of our closest relationships, we are ourselves Pygmalions. Not content with our loved ones' perfectly human differences, we set about to change them, to sculpt them into our conception of what they should be. At first we are attracted by their separate temperaments, intrigued by creatures distinct from ourselves; but the more intimate we grow (and the more we see our loved ones as reflections of ourselves), the more we come to see these differences as imperfections—and the more we assume the responsibility for correcting them. We snipe and criticize, browbeat and bully, we sculpt with guilt and with flattery, with logic and with tears—whatever strategies are most natural to us. Instead of appreciating and nurturing our loved ones' different ways of living, we selfishly try to perfect them into copies of ourselves or our ideals. Not that we do this ceaselessly, nor always maliciously, but all too often, almost without thinking, we fall into this pattern of coercive behavior.

And like Pygmalion, we are inevitably frustrated, for our well-intentioned efforts to make people over only bring us disappointment and conflict. Our loved ones do not—cannot—comply meekly with our coercions, and even if they did we would be taking from them what surely

---

[2] Summarized from Edith Hamilton's *Mythology*, pp. 108-111.

attracted us in the first place, their integrity, their distinct breath of life. Our Pygmalion projects must fail: either our loved ones fight back, and our most intimate relationships become battlegrounds, or our loved ones give in to us, and become as lifeless as Pygmalion's statue. In this paradoxical game, we lose even if we win.

Of course, in the legend, Venus took pity on Pygmalion and brought his statue to life, and he and "Galatea," as he named her, blushed, embraced, and married with the goddess's blessing. The rest of us, however, cannot rely on such miraculous intervention. We must indeed take responsibility for our own relationships, but instead of resorting to coercion, we must try to abandon our Pygmalion projects, by learning, if we can, to understand and to honor our fundamental differences in temperament. If we can respect the right of our loved ones to be different from ourselves—to be perfect in their own ways—then we can begin to bring the beauty of our own relationships alive.

The argument of my books is not entirely new. I take my main title, in fact, from David Keirsey and Marilyn Bates's *Please Understand Me: Character and Temperament Types*, and throughout these pages I am indebted to their wonderfully perceptive analysis of human behavior and relationship styles. However, the nature of my evidence—literary characters—*is* unusual, and needs perhaps a few words of explanation. For if Pygmalion's attempt to shape human life into art was misguided, then the opposite impulse, to see in art the shape of human life, is the very basis of my discussions.

I make at the outset one I hope not too obvious assumption: that the skillful novelist (playwright, poet) and the skillful temperament psychologist are both, of necessity, skillful people-watchers. The cornerstone of realistic fiction has always been the storyteller's astute observation of human behavior. We marvel at how "lifelike" are his characters or how "true-to-life" are their experiences. The so-called "Romantic" and "Symbolist" writers may have loftier visions, but they base their fictions nonetheless on authentic human types before they transcend to their ideal worlds or retreat into their private fantasies. Even such clearly unrealistic forms of fiction as myth and caricature build upon a sharp-eyed perception of human characteristics. Thus the Greek epic heroes, as well as the gods, are plagued with all our human foibles, and Charles Dickens's most grotesque characters embody our most familiar human traits. As one literary critic has put it:

> Literature portrays almost every conceivable human action, thought, attitude, emotion, situation, or problem. In one way or another people are basic to the literary imagination, even in its most fanciful flights.[3]

Certainly fictional characters are not real people, and to insist on their reality may close us off from an author's distinctive view of the world. Still, when a story catches, as Henry James described it, "the very note and trick, the strange irregular rhythm" of human behavior, we know that we are "touching truth" and breathing the "air of

---

[3] B. Bernard Cohen, *Writing About Literature*, p. 37.

reality."[4] In other words, when a story lives for us and catches us up in its artifice, most often it is because we see ourselves and our predicaments in its pages, and such a personal recognition can delight us—or disturb us profoundly—with its insight. Knowing this, Hamlet instructed a troup of actors to catch his uncle's conscience with a play—and defined the power of fiction to make us perceive ourselves more clearly:

> the purpose of playing...was and is, to hold, as 'twere, the mirror up to nature.[5]

In much the same way, the writing of the more perceptive temperament psychologists also unnerves us with this rush of recognition. To read David Keirsey's sixteen character portraits in *Please Understand Me* is to look in a mirror indeed. When I began to edit *Please Understand Me,* I remember browsing ahead in the manuscript and being a little shaken by the air of truth in my own portrait, the "NF" Author, as Keirsey called it then. I felt quite found out at the time, almost as if some novelist or playwright had sketched me in his working notebook. (A decade of reports from *Please Understand Me* readers of all types suggests such unmasking is frequently the case.) I found the other portraits nearly as fascinating (no one is quite as fascinating as oneself), and as I worked on the manuscript I realized that Keirsey's word portraits of Isabel Myers's four-letter designations (the Inspector for Myers's "ISTJ," the Performer for the "ESFP," and so on)

---

[4] Henry James, "The Art of Fiction" in *Partial Portraits,* pp. 398, 390.

[5] William Shakespeare, *Hamlet,* III,ii,19-20.

were offering me an extraordinary instrument: a flexible and surprisingly accurate vocabulary for discussing the welter of human personality.

As with all experience of a new vocabulary, I began to see the world around me with new clarity and in new detail, and very soon my family, my students, my colleagues, friends and foes alike, found their way into the categories of personality I was internalizing. Not that they were reduced from complex, unique individuals, but the broader lines of their attitudes and imperatives came into focus. And in my work—reading and teaching literature—I made a twofold discovery. Not only could I comprehend literary characters with more insight, but I began to see that throughout history the great novelists and playwrights had been bringing to life the same gallery of real life characters that Keirsey was describing in *Please Understand Me*, and in his more recent book, *Portraits of Temperament*. The impulsive "SP" Artisans and the spiritual "NF" Idealists, the logical "NT" Rationals and the dutiful "SJ" Guardians, all kinds and combinations of these characters lived in the pages of Chaucer, Shakespeare, Jane Austen, Dickens, D.H. Lawrence, Hemingway, and many, many more.

To be sure, literary characters give themselves, in most cases, to this sort of category, providing the most amazing illustrations of Keirsey's type portraits. After all, as the critic Robert Scholes has argued, writers create their characters from two impulses: "the impulse to individualize and the impulse to typify."[6] Authors

---

[6] Robert Scholes, *Elements of Literature*, p. 109.

(particularly "NF" Idealist authors) cherish the mystery of the individual and bristle at the idea of putting unique human beings into boxes; but the best of them also admit that their characters typify larger categories of humanity. Indeed, much of the interest (and the charm) of fiction lies in its power to be discriminating and representative at the same time. Thus Henry James cautions us that "Humanity is immense, and reality has a myriad forms,"[7] but he also understands that "Art is essentially selection...whose main care is to be typical."[8] Professional literary critics have long endeavored to unravel characters' unique complexities by means of psychological analysis; temperament theory can now provide us with a finer language (a finer "vocabulary" as I have called it) for recognizing the broader patterns of human behavior, first in the characters and then in ourselves.

My hope in these books, then, is to marry these two characterologies into an informative and I hope entertaining look at the different ways people go about their closest relationships. I want to demonstrate that, by seeing literary characters as discerning portraits of human character styles (Jay Gatsby as an "SP" Artisan, say, or Hamlet as an "NF" Idealist), we can learn a good deal about our own interpersonal games and strategies from literature—and perhaps discover a new interest in literature in the process. In other words, by regarding the lives of literary characters as virtual case studies of the Keirseyan Types, we can, in the mirror of these fictions, better per-

---

[7] Henry James, "The Art of Fiction" in *Partial Portraits*, pp. 387-8.

[8] Henry James, "The Art of Fiction" in *Partial Portraits*, p. 398.

ceive ourselves and our own Pygmalion projects. Which returns me to the topic of my books, potentially the most coercive relationship of all: Love.

Approaching temperament styles through literature in one way broadens the field of research—all of those stories, all of those characters—but it also narrows the focus to those subjects that literature most eloquently addresses. And certainly the subject upon which literature lavishes most attention and reveals most insight is, by far, love. Love, courtship, passion, marriage, this "constant sensitiveness of characters for each other," as E.M. Forster described it, "this constant awareness, this endless readjustment, this ceaseless hunger"[9]—love in all its forms and complications fascinates the literary imagination, and provides a wealth of detail for the reader with an eye for character types. Indeed, the strategies of love so tirelessly pursued in novels and plays amply illustrate Keirsey's portraits of the Artisan, Guardian, Rational, and Idealist mating styles, as well as largely support his theory of the Pygmalion project. For better or for worse, we do seem irresistibly attracted to other types, and we do attempt—and almost invariably with unfortunate consequences—to reshape our loved ones in our own image. This too is the abundant evidence of literature.

Literature and temperament theory thus combined offer us more than either fictitious characters or oversimplified categories. Broadly defined by the temperament

---

[9] E.M. Forster, *Aspects of the Novel*, pp. 54-5.

psychologist and richly detailed by the novelist or playwright, these are *our* relationships, depicting our attractions and regrets, our dreams and strategies, our coercions and compromises. If we will look carefully into the mirror of fiction, we can come to understand ourselves more clearly, and perhaps recognize the Pygmalion in us all.

But first, to those of you unfamiliar with temperament theory, or who have forgotten exactly what all the capital letters ("SP," "NT," etc.) and all the talk about "temperaments" and "types" is about, I want to offer the following diagnostic summary, newly formulated by David Keirsey. You might first want to find the columns, and thus the temperament styles, that best describe you and your loved ones, though certainly a summary knowledge of the four basic styles will help you with my character descriptions in this volume. Remember that the following table is a shorthand classifier; for a more complete personality survey, take Keirsey's Temperament Sorter questionnaire from *Please Understand Me* (reproduced in Appendix B at the back of this book). Remember also that all of us have *all* of these characteristics, and surely many more, and that our temperament is merely a characteristic dominance in our behavior of one style over the others.

Three following pages: ***The Keirsey Brief Temperament Sorter,*** *reproduced by permission of Dr. David Keirsey.*

The Keirsey Brief Temperament Sorter

First: *Quickly glance down each column and decide which column is most descriptive of you.*

Second: *Carefully read across each row and circle one word in each row that applies to you best.*

You Usually ARE:

funloving	respectable	enlightened	intimate
graceful	responsible	ingenious	authentic
experienced	legitimate	scientific	altruistic
impressive	belonging	focused	empathic
excited	serious	resolute	enthusiastic
impulsive	official	rational	ethical
adventurous	secure	insightful	unique
mobile	civilized	independent	fulfilled
sophisticated	patient	objective	mystical
daring	unselfish	competent	benevolent

You Usually DO:

rehearsing	factfinding	theorizing	predicting
artifacting	recording	philosophizing	metaphorizing
composing	insuring	architecting	conciliating
concretizing	measuring	categorizing	idealizing
promoting	supervising	marshalling	teaching
playing	providing	inventing	revealing
approximating	particularizing	generalizing	guessing
varying	standardizing	differentiating	integrating
effecting	inspecting	controlling	divining
expediting	itemizing	explaining	implying
Artisan Type	**Guardian Type**	**Rational Type**	**Idealist Type**

The largest column sum may indicate your primary temperament, the second largest, your secondary temperament. Hopefully, your first impression from the columns is consistent with your word selection from the rows. If not, you might profit from asking others to study your actions and tell you what they see for, say, six months, and then take the test again.

The Keirsey Brief Temperament Sorter

First: *Quickly glance down each column and decide which column is most descriptive of you.*

Second: *Carefully read across each row and circle one word in each row that applies to you best.*

You Usually ARE:

funloving	respectable	enlightened	intimate
graceful	responsible	ingenious	authentic
experienced	legitimate	scientific	altruistic
impressive	belonging	focused	empathic
excited	serious	resolute	enthusiastic
impulsive	official	rational	ethical
adventurous	secure	insightful	unique
mobile	civilized	independent	fulfilled
sophisticated	patient	objective	mystical
daring	unselfish	competent	benevolent

You Usually DO:

rehearsing	factfinding	theorizing	predicting
artifacting	recording	philosophizing	metaphorizing
composing	insuring	architecting	conciliating
concretizing	measuring	categorizing	idealizing
promoting	supervising	marshalling	teaching
playing	providing	inventing	revealing
approximating	particularizing	generalizing	guessing
varying	standardizing	differentiating	integrating
effecting	inspecting	controlling	divining
expediting	itemizing	explaining	implying
☐	☐	☐	☐
Artisan Type	**Guardian Type**	**Rational Type**	**Idealist Type**

The largest column sum may indicate your primary temperament, the second largest, your secondary temperament. Hopefully, your first impression from the columns is consistent with your word selection from the rows. If not, you might profit from asking others to study your actions and tell you what they see for, say, six months, and then take the test again.

The Keirsey Brief Temperament Sorter

First: *Quickly glance down each column and decide which column is most descriptive of you.*

Second: *Carefully read across each row and circle one word in each row that applies to you best.*

You Usually ARE:

funloving	respectable	enlightened	intimate
graceful	responsible	ingenious	authentic
experienced	legitimate	scientific	altruistic
impressive	belonging	focused	empathic
excited	serious	resolute	enthusiastic
impulsive	official	rational	ethical
adventurous	secure	insightful	unique
mobile	civilized	independent	fulfilled
sophisticated	patient	objective	mystical
daring	unselfish	competent	benevolent

You Usually DO:

rehearsing	factfinding	theorizing	predicting
artifacting	recording	philosophizing	metaphorizing
composing	insuring	architecting	conciliating
concretizing	measuring	categorizing	idealizing
promoting	supervising	marshalling	teaching
playing	providing	inventing	revealing
approximating	particularizing	generalizing	guessing
varying	standardizing	differentiating	integrating
effecting	inspecting	controlling	divining
expediting	itemizing	explaining	implying
☐	☐	☐	☐
Artisan Type	**Guardian Type**	**Rational Type**	**Idealist Type**

The largest column sum may indicate your primary temperament, the second largest, your secondary temperament. Hopefully, your first impression from the columns is consistent with your word selection from the rows. If not, you might profit from asking others to study your actions and tell you what they see for, say, six months, and then take the test again.

Chapter 1 Dionysus Bound

Dionysus, son of Zeus, consummate god,
most terrible, and yet most gentle, to mankind.

—Euripides[1]

Of the four personality temperaments elaborated by David Keirsey in *Please Understand Me,* the Artisan temperament would appear least inclined to pursue a Pygmalion project. The totem deity of the Artisans is Dionysus, the god of Fertility and Revelry—and Wine—and certainly Dionysus seems more in his element enlivening a party or performing in the bedroom than manipulating his partner into psychological shape. Indeed, Keirsey observed that one Artisan, the Composer, as he named him, is of all the types "most likely to 'let be'" his or her loved ones, evincing little "intent or desire to change the spouse."[2] This *laissez faire* attitude toward love in some degree marks all the Artisans, and makes a coercive, agenda-laden relationship seem virtually out of character.

---

[1] Euripides, *The Bacchae,* William Arrowsmith, trans., p. 231.

[2] David Keirsey and Marilyn Bates, *Please Understand Me,* p. 77.

To be sure, Artisans (called "SP"s by Myers) are by nature impulsive, spontaneous, and free-spirited; they thrive on action, movement, and excitement, and are exceptionally generous and fraternal, cheerful and artistic. To the Artisan, life is a sensual feast to be savored fully and shared freely with others. The Artisan is thus Chaucer's Franklin (*i.e.* country gentleman):

> A sanguine man, high-coloured and benign,
> He loved a morning sop of cake in wine.
> He lived for pleasure and had always done,
> For he was Epicurus' very son,
> In whose opinion sensual delight
> Was the one true felicity in sight.[3]

And he is Shakespeare's riotous Sir Toby Belch, who brushes aside Malvolio's snide admonitions with the famous question,

> Dost thou think, because thou art virtuous,
> there shall be no more cakes and ale?[4]

Artisans, as well, are particularly bold and insubordinate, loving to take chances and to push their luck, risking everything to go their own way. They live by their wits, in the moment, easily bored by other people's rules, and often unable to resist puncturing others' pretensions. The Artisan is Henry Fielding's quintessential rascal, Tom Jones, who delights in enraging his pious tutors (aptly named Messrs. "Thwackum" and "Square")

---

[3] Geoffrey Chaucer, *The Canterbury Tales*, Nevill Coghill trans., p. 29.

[4] William Shakespeare, *Twelfth Night*, II,iii,117-18.

by ridiculing his self-righteous half brother. Tom, intones the fastidious narrator,

> was indeed a thoughtless, giddy youth, with little sobriety in his manners and less in his countenance; and would often very impudently and indecently laugh at his companion for his serious behavior.[5]

He is also Shakespeare's most notorious reveller and con-man, Falstaff, whose crafty sense of fun is legendary and infectious:

> I am not only witty in myself,
> but the cause that wit is in other men.[6]

As a rule, Artisans prefer to minimize their responsibilities, ties, and obligations, and they will avoid interpersonal tensions and complications whenever possible. Well thought out goals or deep emotional commitments to person or to place—anything that restricts the whim or binds the moment—frustrate the Artisans and burden their carefree nature. The Artisan is Bernard Shaw's Alfred Doolittle, who insists he will take no more than a fiver from Henry Higgins:

> No governor....Ten pounds is a lot of money: it makes a man feel prudent like; and then good-bye to happiness.[7]

---

[5] Henry Fielding, *Tom Jones*, p. 90.

[6] William Shakespeare, *Henry IV, Part Two*, I,ii,9-10.

[7] George Bernard Shaw, *Pygmalion*, p. 50.

He is John Steinbeck's paisano, Danny, whose childlike existence is changed forever, "weighed down with the responsibility of ownership," when he inherits two small houses on Tortilla Flat:

> Before he ever went to look at his property he bought a gallon of red wine and drank most of it himself....No more in life would that face be free of care....His shoulders straightened to withstand the complexity of life.[8]

The Artisan is thus a whole cast of Dionysian characters in all kinds of fictions. He is Sancho Panza, Huckleberry Finn, and the dashing James Bond; he is Cool Hand Luke in the film (who admitted, "I never planned a thing in my life"), the mischievous Papagena in Mozart's *The Magic Flute*, and Dickens's cleverest pickpocket, the Artful Dodger; he is Hemingway's noble old man and the sea, the wise-cracking Hawkeye Pierce in *M*A*S*H* (particularly in Robert Altman's original film), and Oscar Madison, the lovable slob in Neil Simon's *The Odd Couple*. The female Artisan is Chaucer's worldly Wife of Bath, Molly Bloom in James Joyce's *Ulysses,* and the bubbly younger daughters in *Pride and Prejudice* (who have "high animal spirits, and a sort of natural self-consequence"[9]); she is Shakespeare's merry wives of Windsor, Bizet's fiery Carmen, and *Gone with the Wind's* Scarlett O'Hara; she is Flaubert's Emma Bovary, Nabokov's nymphette Lolita, and the irrepressible Miss Piggy.

---

[8] John Steinbeck, *Tortilla Flat*, pp. 5, 12.

[9] Jane Austen, *Pride and Prejudice*, p. 33.

The question, to return, is how this impulsive, free-wheeling, "live and let live" temperament style can entangle itself in a coercive Pygmalion project. If the Artisans' natural impulse is toward open, generous action—easy come, easy go—how can they narrow themselves to criticize and maneuver their loved ones? Again, if their instinct is to avoid complicated, scheming relationships (Artisans might call them "sticky" relationships), how can they devote themselves to the tenacious infighting needed to manipulate another person? The answer is that *all* people have it in them to be Pygmalions, and Artisans—despite the apparent contradiction—are no exception. To their credit, some Artisans may be less inclined to such coercive behavior than the rest of us, and some may be less conscious, less deliberate about their plans for their loved ones. But the evidence from literature suggests that, in the wrong relationships, Artisans are fully capable, even masterly, sculptors—after all, was not Pygmalion himself presumably an Artisan? The best that can be said is that in comfortable relationships, with sufficient breathing room, Artisans can resist a Pygmalion project more easily than the other temperaments. (While interference with our loved ones comes almost naturally to the rest of us, the Artisan's nature is indeed to live and let live.) Nevertheless, when trapped in a binding, chafing relationship, stifled and bored, the Artisans find themselves with the same two options as the rest of us: to walk away or to chip away. In other words, when Dionysus finds himself in chains, he can either break free and move on, or he can struggle to reshape his loved one to his satisfaction. Unlike the other temperaments, Artisans appear particularly artful at both scenarios.

To be or not to be a Pygmalion is, then, a significant question for the Artisans, and their choice of tactics breaks quite clearly along lines of type and of gender. First of all, throughout literature, the Players (called "SFP"s by Myers) appear on average less manipulative than their cousins, the Operators (Myers's "STP"s). Keirsey helps explain the matter, identifying the Players by their sensual, playful nature.[10] Players are life's hedonists, considering pleasure as the true purpose of life. Players want life to be fun, want to have a good time, and they delight and often seduce others with their joy of living in the moment. Players approach life as a game or a performance, to be enjoyed or perfected, but not to be taken too seriously. Life is an entertainment, a banquet, an adventure, filled with grace, variety, and daring. This almost childlike delight in the immediate, sensual world infuses a spontaneous generosity into the Players' relationships. They share whatever they have with loved ones and strangers alike; they are particularly sensitive to others' suffering (which is precisely the *loss* of joy); and they are exceptionally kind to others, showing a special affinity with children and animals, who seem naturally close to the Players' unconscious style of living. Indeed, in one sense, the Player is a large, friendly puppy gambolling and frisking its way through people's lives, offering unconditional and undiscriminating love, then moving on if threatened with collar and leash.

---

[10] David Keirsey, *Portraits of Temperament*, p. 31.

Clearly, this sort of Artisan resorts to a Pygmalion project only in the most repressive circumstances.

The Operators, on the other hand, seem by nature more competitive and manipulative in their relationships. Keirsey characterizes them as "Operators" not only because they operate the concrete "things" (tools, machines, instruments, weapons) of this world with innate skill, but because Operators (particularly the extraverted Operators) can also operate people with amazing virtuosity.[11] Although just as impulsive and nearly as excitable as Players, Operators are tougher of mind—victory, not sensual pleasure, is their first joy in life. Keirsey emphasizes this shrewd aggressiveness: Operators will

> do or say whatever they have to to get their way. They are not out to please...but are competitive, seeking to outdo, overtake, outmaneuver, or best whomever they contest.... Operators would rather outsmart others than please them; not that they are averse to giving pleasure, but that being top dog is more important.[12]

Operators don't so much entertain others as make use of them, manipulating people, like tools, with artistic virtuosity. They are generally more assertive in relationships than the Players, quite charming and comfortable making the first interpersonal move, and extraverted Operators actually feast on the give and take of politics

---

[11] David Keirsey, *Portraits of Temperament*, p. 18.

[12] David Keirsey, *Portraits of Temperament*, p. 19.

and negotiations. In short, Operators and Players both see relationships as a game, but while the Players play to enjoy, the Operators play to win. Brash, crafty, contentious, resourceful, certainly more a fox than a puppy, the Operator has all the skills needed to excel in the most intimate tactics of coercing a loved one, molding him or her to a personal vision. In literature, if an Artisan character has taken up a serious Pygmalion project, chances are he or she is an Operator.

The evidence from literature suggests one other important distinction: characters engaging in Pygmalion projects, be they Players or Operators, are likely to be female. This gender link clearly reflects male authors' long-held anti-feminist bias. Basing their attitude on the story of Eve's tempting Adam, western writers have traditionally—and unfairly—seen women as the weaker and therefore more scheming and manipulative sex. The virtuous, unsuspecting male is seduced by the conniving female—the scenario is sadly familiar. But even more than implying some genetic predisposition, I think literature is reflecting the social roles assigned to men and women by western societies. If the Artisans' choice in a relationship is to break free and walk away, or to remain bound in the relationship and cope, then clearly Artisan men have a greater license in our culture to abandon their ties, while Artisan women are constrained more frequently to the role of Pygmalion. Western culture has always afforded men more freedom to live on impulse, to wield the tool or the weapon, to explore and to conquer the world—all thoroughly Artisan behaviors. Women's "natural" place, until very recently at least, has been in the home, raising children, or (to oversimplify) in such nurturing and conscientious careers as nurse, teacher, or secretary. In other words, men have been encouraged to be wandering, gambling, impulsive Artisans, while women by and large have been firmly fixed in the smaller world of domestic responsibility.

This division of roles would only make sense if all Artisans were men, while all responsible, conserving types ("SJ" Guardians, as I will describe in Volume Two) were women. But women who also happen to be Artisans have traditionally had fewer opportunities to express their Dionysian temperament, and so many have been forced to live vicariously, through their relationships, manipulating—or sculpting—the men in their lives to provide the excitement denied them by their culture. Artisan men conquer the world; Artisan women stay home and conquer their men. Of course, some extraordinary women have defied society's constraints and lived daring Artisan lives as athletes, artists, aviators, entertainers, and so on. But far more frequently literature tells the story of Artisan women resorting to a Pygmalion project to carve out some social impact, some semblance of psychological potency. Fortunately, in recent decades, Artisan women have found much greater freedom to live and work and mate as they wish, and the serious literature of the last century—Henrik Ibsen's *Hedda Gabler* a disturbing example—has explored the repression of the Artisan woman in our culture as a tragic theme.

One last irony before turning to the literature. Why don't Artisans just avoid complicated commitments?

Why not simply remain free agents in their relationships and preclude Pygmalion projects altogether? Research in temperament theory, as well as the evidence of serious literature, suggests quite a surprising answer. Many Artisans, instead of preferring spontaneous and free relationships, seem instinctively drawn to their opposites, the responsible and safely anchored "SJ" Guardians.[13] Perhaps seeking stability, perhaps asking forgiveness for their waywardness, perhaps just needing someone to take care of them—whatever the case, Artisans in life and in literature frequently choose a mate whose way of living is sooner or later contentious with their own. Not that all Artisan-Guardian relationships are unworkable, or even unhappy. As long as the couple's unavoidable conflicts between impulse and deliberation, insubordination and duty, and spending and saving are not too bitter, Artisan-Guardian mates can often find a comfortable balance, settling the Artisan down a bit, and helping loosen up the Guardian. In many cases, the marriage takes on the amiable stasis of a mischievous child and a stern but understanding parent. The casual coercion in such a relationship may even be enjoyable up to a certain point: the Artisan needs someone to surprise, and the Guardian needs someone to correct.

But if the tension between these opposites becomes too severe, too humorless, then the Pygmalion projects can become urgent and retaliatory, turning into ugly struggles for power, pitting Artisan gestures of irresponsibility against Guardian complaining and ridicule. In desperate

---

[13] David Keirsey and Marilyn Bates, *Please Understand Me*, pp. 76-79.

cases (when unable to escape the relationship), the Artisan may even escalate the psychological battle into physical abuse, or may try to spur the sober Guardian spouse into spontaneous action with binges of extravagance, dissipation, or infidelity. Again, the female Artisan bears the heavier burden. Not as free to sever her ties, indeed, usually consigned to the sedate Guardian role in the relationship, the female Artisan is more liable to pursue her Pygmalion project into these extremes of sado-masochistic manipulation, punishing herself or her Guardian partner in some way as a means of shaping the relationship. Martha in *Who's Afraid of Virginia Woolf?* is a terrifying depiction of such purposeful destructiveness, finally screaming to her Guardian husband George the truth of their "vile, crushing" marriage: "My arm has gotten tired of whipping you."[14] Unhappily, far too many Artisan females in Victorian and modern literature share some level of Martha's desperation.

To keep this in perspective, however: in real life, most Artisans go about love in a far simpler, far less malicious way. Literature of the last century has accurately characterized the Artisans' sado-masochistic darker side, but has surely overemphasized the Artisans' resort to such abusive tactics, just as it has dwelt inordinately on the malaise of twentieth century life, what Thomas Hardy called "the ache of modernism."[15] In any event, Player

---

[14] Edward Albee, *Who's Afraid of Virginia Woolf?*, p. 153. For a brilliant examination of George and Martha's punishing marital manipulations, see Paul Watzlawick, Janet Beavin, and Don Jackson's *Pragmatics of Human Communication*, pp. 149-186.

[15] Thomas Hardy, *Tess of the D'Urbervilles*, p. 140.

or Operator, male or female, Pygmalion or not, the Artisans are a favorite subject of novelists and playwrights, and—forgiving a certain penchant for dramatic extreme—literature has much of depth and value to reveal about them.

Let me add, finally, that the following chapters reflect one further division among the Artisans, roughly coinciding with Myers's distinction between "introvert" and "extravert." I distinguish between the *seclusive* Players (whom I call the Sensualists) and the *gregarious* Players (called the Performers); and I distinguish between the *seclusive* Operators (the Instrumentalists) and the *gregarious* Operators (the Promoters). As you can see, such subdividing can easily become confusing; and therefore, since I've always found genealogies helpful in complicated novels and plays (keeping the two Cathys straight in *Wuthering Heights*, for example, or the royal families in Shakespeare), I want to offer this visual guide to the types and subtypes of Artisans analyzed in my pages:

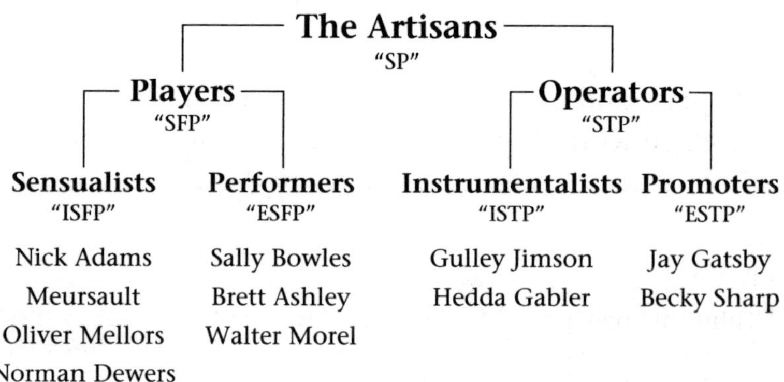

Chapter 2
The Sensualist

> *He wanted to take away from her all her effort, all that seemed her very* raison d'être. *He wanted to make her submit, yield, blindly pass away out of all her strenuous consciousness.*
>
> —D.H. Lawrence[1]

Keirsey characterizes the introverted, feeling Artisan (whom Myers called the "ISFP") as the "Artist" in *Please Understand Me,* and then as the "Composer" in *Portraits of Temperament,* trying in both names to capture the quiet artisanship of the type. Novelists and playwrights, on the other hand, most often depict the artist as an "NF" Idealist, soulfully searching for (or sometimes prophesying) the abstract truths of existence—discovering some profound meaning in life—rather than as a fundamentally unconscious, inarticulate craftsman of concrete reality.[2] And so, hoping not to complicate matters too

---

[1] D.H. Lawrence, *The Fox*, p. 178.

[2] Think of such philosophical fine artists as Paul Morel in D.H Lawrence's *Sons and Lovers*, Eugene Witla in Theodore Dreiser's *The "Genius,"* Jude Fawley in Thomas Hardy's *Jude the Obscure*, or Goldmund in Hermann Hesse's *Narcissus and Goldmund.*

much more, I have chosen a third name, "Sensualist," to describe this first type of Artisan as he is portrayed in literature, more an artist of the flesh and of earth than of spirit or of consciousness, and not so much even a painter, dancer, or composer, but a soft-spoken (though often mischievous) master of the natural world, of the body, and of sexual pleasure.

Nick Adams

Nick Adams, Ernest Hemingway's alter-ego in his earliest short stories, feels he must break off with Marjorie, his first, adolescent love, but he doesn't know how or why. In "The End of Something," on a nightfall fishing trip, Nick and Marjorie set their trout lines, build a campfire, and sit in silence, watching the moon rise above the lake. Marjorie, a serious, attentive "SJ" Guardian, finally (and shyly) asks what's the matter, and there follows a brief scene of inarticulate separation:

> "What's really the matter?"
>
> "I don't know."
>
> "Go on and say it."
>
> Nick looked on at the moon, coming up over the hills.
>
> "It isn't fun anymore."
>
> He was afraid to look at Marjorie. Then he looked at her. She sat there with her back toward him. He looked at her back. "It isn't fun anymore. Not any of it."
>
> She didn't say anything. He went on. "I feel as though everything was gone to hell inside of me. I don't know, Marge. I don't know what to say."

> He looked on at her back.
> "Isn't love any fun?" Marjorie said.
> "No," Nick said.[3]

This may be a somber introduction to a portrait of what I have described as a light-hearted, hedonistic Dionysian, but Hemingway's scene is a good place to begin, raising two fundamental issues about love for the Sensualists.

First of all, Sensualists insist that love be, to use Nick's term, "fun." Nick had first befriended Marjorie for the good-natured, essentially fraternal pleasure of sharing his know-how, teaching her all about boating and fishing, about the sky at night and camping in the woods—Sensualists are hunters by instinct, and often become expert outdoorsmen. Nick was flattered by Marjorie's quiet devotion, and as he drew closer to her, he fell into an unwitting Pygmalion project, gently shaping Marjorie into his mirror image. And the results of his sculpting are predictable: once Marjorie had mastered all Nick's skills, becoming nearly his equal, his affection for her turned into boredom and impatience. A bit earlier in the scene Nick had come to the real point, criticizing Marjorie for having learned his skills too well: "You know everything. That's the trouble. You know you do...I've taught you everything." Nick is young and confused about his feelings; he knows there is nothing actually wrong with Marjorie—if anything she is a more perfect companion now than before—and he can't understand his own selfishness. But Nick is a Sensualist with a stagnant relationship on his hands; for some reason (now that the

---

[3] Ernest Hemingway, *In Our Time*, pp. 34-35.

Pygmalion project is complete) he is no longer having "fun" with Marjorie and, even though it bothers him, the urge to break away is overpowering.

Nick's behavior may be new and puzzling to him, but is quite typical of the Sensualists. Keirsey calls the Sensualists the "Seclusive Players"[4] for their instinctive sense of privacy, but "seclusive" does not imply "serious" or "reclusive." Sensualists are unmistakeably "Players" who want love to be fun, and this means filled with sensual variety and spontaneity. Though they can appear quite detached, and do withdraw at times to perfect their skills, Sensualists—like all the Artisans—come to life around other people and see interpersonal relations as an exhilarating game. Indeed, Sensualists love almost for their own amusement—impulsively, impetuously—and are most intrigued when the loved one is unknown and the pattern of interaction is unfamiliar. Much like a dancer improvising a new routine or a sculptor fingering a new block of marble, Sensualists are happiest discovering a new affection or exploring the fresh texture of a new relationship. This is their "fun," the surprise and delight of unexpected sensations, and this can make them captivating companions, charming the lives they enter with their playfulness and their excitement. But as Marjorie finds out in "The End of Something," Sensualists usually don't wear well in long relationships, or in relationships that grow too entangling. They soon lose interest when their lives become predictable or tied down;

---

[4] David Keirsey, *Portraits of Temperament,* p. 41.

the thrill of discovery is over and they can do little but escape the routine and move on to the next experience, even if saddened by the farewell, as Nick clearly is in Hemingway's story.

Nick's inability—or his reluctance—to put his feelings into words is also typical of Sensualists, and is often a source of frustration for their loved ones. Nick refers to his relationship with Marjorie as "it" throughout the scene, and Hemingway, himself a close-mouthed Sensualist, entitled the story the end of "Something," as if spoken from Nick's uncertainty. Nick may be young and unsure of his feelings, of course, but his reticence suggests more than an adolescent shyness. When speaking of manual skills, such as cleaning their bait-fish, Nick is precise and firmly directive: "You don't want to take the ventral fin out," he cautions Marjorie as they set their lines; "It'll be all right for bait but it's better with the ventral fin in." To describe his emotional confusion, however, he can only stumble with the vague confession: "I don't know, Marge. I don't know what to say."

Nick's shy silence may have several causes. Sensualists introspect so rarely that their feelings often take them by surprise, finding little articulate expression except in action. But perhaps Nick is also trying to be kind to Marjorie. He is no hard-edged Operator willing to throw Marjorie over with glib excuses. As a Sensualist he senses her pain, and perhaps tries to soften the blow with his tongue-tied regrets. Or possibly Nick is hoping to obscure his own responsibility for the hurt, a familiar Sensualist tactic in times of stress. In a companion story, "The Three-Day Blow," Nick gets drunk with his buddy Bill trying to numb Marjorie's memory. But unable to drink away the "hell inside" him, he tries again to deny any blame: "All of a sudden everything was over....I don't know why it was. I couldn't help it. Just like when the three-day blows come now and rip all the leaves off the trees."[5] Nick finds some absolution in this simile, the force of nature (as well as the whiskey) helping him accept that all things have their inevitable conclusion. But *why* he must leave Marjorie is still very much a mystery to him.

Certainly, Nick feels trapped in his relationship with Marjorie, frightened of a more serious commitment. He carefully avoids the word "love" throughout the dialogue, and the weight of his silence finally forces Marjorie to voice his underlying apprehension: "isn't love any fun?" For Nick, the adolescent fun of falling in love (and of shaping the loved one) is over and he has come to that crossroads where he must either acknowledge a more faithful, entangling bond with Marjorie, or leave her behind. Both courses are painful to him (Hemingway, for all his simple words, is not a simplistic writer), but even though Nick is sensitive enough to feel the sting of this dilemma, as a Sensualist he has little instinct but to escape. Like one of his trout fighting the hook, pumping against the current, Nick is aware of little but that he must act in some way to free himself. This is not to say that Sensualists are devoid of conscience or are incapable

[5] Ernest Hemingway, *In Our Time*, p. 47.

of fidelity. Indeed, as Nick's ambivalence in the scene suggests, Sensualists can commit to their relationships quite sincerely, and will put up with more disappointment—and more manipulation—from their loved ones than most other Artisans. But though Sensualists may tolerate their captivity with considerable patience, more than likely they are biding their time, chafing in their psychological chains, and waiting for their chance to break free.

In one sense, however, Hemingway himself lets Nick off the hook. Nick is surely too young to settle in love—on that, most of us can agree. No matter how right for Nick Marjorie may appear in the story (and Hemingway makes her virtually ideal), Nick is wise not to tie himself down so early in life. But temperament theory reminds us that the same might be said of most Artisans, young or old. As Hemingway himself so amply illustrated in his own lifelong quest for danger and romance, freedom of impulse is the very breath of life to the Artisan, regardless of age.

Meursault

In their pursuit of "fun," Sensualists often seem to others to have a distant air about them, something slightly impersonal and self-centered, as if their pleasure in a relationship is the important thing, not their partner. Sensualists can be wonderfully sympathetic and kind, it is true, but their sympathy and kindness often seem indiscriminate, promiscuous, as if offered more for the pleasure of the giving than out of concern for the other person. And while Sensualists may love energetically, they are instinctively cautious about personal obligation, loving for the fun of it, the sensual play, quite content to avoid the normal responsibilities of marriage and family. Meursault, the existential antihero in Albert Camus's *The Stranger*, illustrates all of these ideas (to an almost pathological extreme[6]), kindly accomodating almost everyone in the novel, but oddly disturbing them with his blank indifference to their personal concerns. In an eerie scene with his new girlfriend, a young Guardian with matrimony on her mind, Meursault politely overturns the "serious matter" of marriage:

> Marie came that evening and asked me if I'd marry her. I said I didn't mind; if she was keen on it, we'd get married.
>
> Then she asked me again if I loved her. I replied, much as before, that her question meant nothing or next to nothing—but I supposed I didn't.
>
> "If that's how you feel," she said, "why marry me?"
>
> I explained that it had no importance really, but, if it would give her pleasure, we could get married right away. I pointed out that, anyhow, the suggestion came from her; as for me, I'd merely said, "Yes."
>
> Then she remarked that marriage was a serious matter.
>
> To which I answered: "No."

---

[6] Indeed, Meursault's behavior uncannily illustrates many of the characteristics of the psychopathic personality, as described in Hervey Cleckley's definitive study, *The Mask of Sanity*.

> She kept silent after that, staring at me in a curious way. Then she asked:
>
> "Suppose another girl had asked you to marry her—I mean, a girl you liked in the same way as you like me—would you have said 'Yes' to her, too?"
>
> "Naturally."[7]

Meursault, to be sure, suffers much more difficult questioning later on in *The Stranger,* when he goes on trial for murdering an Arab, shooting him five times with "benign indifference." But his matter-of-fact responses to Marie in this earlier scene help us, in their own curious way, to see more deeply into the nature of love for the Sensualist, and into the very nature of Sensualist consciousness.

Meursault is so indifferent to love because his relation to Marie, and to the world as a whole, is so purely sensual. Very nearly the archtypal Sensualist, Meursault sees almost no spiritual or moral dimension in human relationships. His famous first words in the novel, "Mother died today. Or, maybe yesterday; I can't be sure," immediately establish his deadpan tone, reducing normal family affection to its most factual terms. And even romantic love to Meursault is not a sacred feeling for one person, nor is marriage an eternal commitment witnessed by God. "Love" in this traditional sense means "next to nothing" to Meursault, and his patiently honest replies to Marie's questions make him appear cold-blooded, or as the prosecutor in his trial (an outraged

[7] Albert Camus, *The Stranger,* pp. 52-53.

Guardian) self-righteously concludes: he "had no soul, there was nothing human about [him], not one of those moral qualities which normal men possess had any place in [his] mentality."

In fact, the prosecutor is right, Meursault has no soul, if by "soul" he means any abstract (or spiritual) center to him. Still, to give him credit, Meursault *is* a warm person, quite passionate and responsive, and only seems inhuman and immoral because his love is so solidly anchored in his senses. Although Meursault has difficulty (much like Nick Adams) bringing himself to say the abstract word "love," he is fascinated throughout the novel by the feel of "Marie's stomach rising and falling" under his weight, "the smell of brine that Marie's head had left on the pillow," the look of "her suntanned face...like a velvety brown flower," or the sound of her laugh, which makes him "always want to kiss her." Meursault loves Marie for the sensual excitement she brings him, but has only passing interest in what she thinks or cares about; he's more interested in how her flesh feels—her skin's texture—than how she "feels" as a person, emotionally.

Of course, Meursault tries as best he can to satisfy Marie's more religious, traditional sense of love, even consenting to marry her if it will keep her happy; but his consent is purely practical, pledging little personal devotion—as he says, he would agree to marry anyone he "liked in the same way." Along the same lines, as he and Marie walk to their favorite restaurant, Meursault admires the women they pass on the street:

> The women were good-lookers, and I asked Marie if she, too, noticed this. She said, "Yes," and that she saw what I meant. After that we said nothing for some minutes.[8]

Sensualists are known to infuriate their dates or spouses by openly paying attention to attractive strangers, and indeed, Marie (fuming with jealousy) refuses dinner, and even tries to make Meursault jealous in turn by claiming she has another date that evening. But Meursault meant to be neither cruel nor coy; he was not flirting so much as simply—and quite unconsciously—appreciating the sensual variety around him, very much as a painter observes the beauty of color and contour in the natural world. Whatever catches Meursault's eye seems to fill his awareness for the moment, indiscriminately, and he is absurdly unaware of how callous and promiscuous this makes him appear.

In his own way, certainly, Meursault *is* devoted to Marie, and remembers her fondly in times of extraordinary stress. During his trial, Meursault closes his ears to the prosecutor's endless discussion of "my 'soul,' and the rest of it," and calls to mind sensual images

> of a life which was mine no longer and had once provided me with the surest, humblest pleasures: warm smells of summer, my favorite streets, the sky at evening, Marie's dresses and her laugh.[9]

---

[8] Albert Camus, *The Stranger*, p. 54.

[9] Albert Camus, *The Stranger*, p. 132.

And later in jail, awaiting the guillotine, when the chaplain urges him to confess his sin and see "a divine face" on the stone wall of his cell, Meursault admits that

> once upon a time, perhaps, I used to try to see a face. But it was a sun-gold face, lit up with desire—Marie's face.[10]

With his Sensualist's imagination, Meursault has a much better chance of remembering Marie's face, an object of sensual desire, than of picturing Christ's face, an image of spiritual salvation—but even Marie's face is beyond him: "I'd never seen it, and now I'd given up trying." In short, Meursault would marry Marie for the physical satisfaction, but as such an extreme Sensualist he is virtually incapable of loving her as she would wish it, in Guardian style, earnestly and conscientiously.

Meursault's indifference to any but sensual love helps explain the Sensualist's difficulty with language (remember Nick's inarticulateness in "The End of Something"). Language, in the first place, is an abstract system Sensualists use uncomfortably at best. Words are not sensual things, unless treated as pure sound; they are names of things, meanings, symbols by which we recognize physical things and manipulate them in consciousness. In some sense (as many twentieth century poets believe), language separates us from objects, substituting subjective, abstract symbols—"lies" as the poets would have it—for the concrete things they name. "No ideas but in things" is William Carlos Williams's famous principle

---

[10] Albert Camus, *The Stranger*, p. 149.

for poetry, which suggests that as long as we describe concrete reality with abstract language, we are removed (literally "abstracted") from the physical world, estranged from "the thing itself," by the illusions of consciousness.[11] The physical world, however, is the Sensualists' natural domain, and they seem instinctively suspicious of all words, but particularly the more abstract or spiritual. Thus Nick Adams doesn't know how to explain his ambivalent feelings to Marjorie, and Meursault responds minimally to Marie's desire for love and marriage, in single words, in monosyllables, or says nothing at all.

Hemingway (whose style Camus admitted emulating) describes the Sensualist's mistrust of abstract language in a famous passage from *A Farewell to Arms*:

> I was always embarrassed by the words sacred, glorious, and sacrifice and the expression in vain. We had heard them...now for a long time, and I had seen nothing sacred, and the things that were glorious had no glory and the sacrifices were like the stockyards at Chicago if nothing was done with the meat except to bury it. There were many words you could not stand to hear and finally only the names of places had dignity. Certain numbers were the same way and certain dates and these with the names of the places were all you could say and have them mean anything. Abstract words such as glory, honor, courage, or hallow were obscene beside the concrete names of villages, the numbers of roads, the names of rivers, the numbers of regiments and the dates.[12]

---

[11] See the Appendix: "A Note on Artisan Poetry."

[12] Ernest Hemingway, *A Farewell to Arms*, pp. 184-185.

World War I stripped away many a soldier's grand illusions,[13] to be sure, but in or out of war, Hemingway's many tightlipped Sensualists seem virtually born with this cynical view of words and the hard realities they obscure. And in the same way Meursault, content in the world of his senses, unwilling to exaggerate his feelings with meaningless language, frustrates Marie with the candor of his silence: "Well, I rarely have anything much to say. So naturally I keep my mouth shut."

However, Meursault's indifference to abstraction raises another more subtle issue—the Sensualist's utter incomprehension of time. Just as language abstracts "things" into ideas, inevitably separating us from concrete objects, so time separates us from the concrete "now," abstracting moments into the mental images of past or future. And just as Sensualists, more than any other type, stay close to unconscious, physical reality by simplifying their language, so they live more fully in the moment, the sensual "now," by entertaining a minimal conception of time. In *The Stranger*, with amazing insight, Camus explains Meursault's curious insensitivity

---

[13] For Hemingway's definitive disillusioned soldier, read his eerie story, "Soldier's Home," from *In Our Time*. Note the soldier's almost painfully flattened consciousness as he sits on his parents' porch after the war, observing with an artist's eye the hometown girls:

> He did not want any consequences. He did not want any consequences ever again. He wanted to live along without consequences....Now he would have liked a girl if she had come to him and not wanted to talk. But here at home it was all too complicated....He liked the girls that were walking along the other side of the street....He would like to have one of them. But it was not worth it. They were such a nice pattern. He liked the pattern. It was exciting. But he would not go through all the talking (pp. 71-72).

to abstract moral issues as essentially an unawareness of time. Questioned by the prosecutor in his trial if he regretted murdering the Arab, Meursault admits,

> I didn't feel much regret for what I'd done. Still...I'd have liked to have a chance of explaining to him, in a quite friendly, almost affectionate way, that I have never been able really to regret anything in all my life. I've always been far too absorbed in the present moment, or the immediate future, to think back.[14]

This point is vital to understand the Sensualists, indeed, all the Artisans: they live so completely in the present moment, their senses so fully involved in the details of immediate reality, that they are nearly oblivious to past and future. This living on the razor's edge of time is at the heart of the most characteristic Artisan behavior. Strangers to the past, they are usually uninterested in the sins of the past, only annoyed by the voice of conscience or guilt; nor do they pay particular attention to the lessons of the past, preserved in history, tradition, and law. For most Artisans, what's done is done, and dwelling on past experience is a boring waste of time. (Sensualist fine artists, for example, rarely talk about their work after finishing it.) Strangers as well to the long term future, Artisans are uncomfortable living for tomorrow, quickly bored by goal-setting, commitment, practice, anything that requires their perseverence; nor do they particularly fear the future, boldly refusing to heed warnings or to calculate risk. But the immediate future?

---

[14] Albert Camus, *The Stranger*, pp. 126-127.

Here Artisans thrive, enjoying just enough sense of time to give full play to their gambling spirit, their absolute certainty that the next try will bring them luck. And the present moment, the "now"? Here Artisans are virtuosos, living with an unconscious command of action that delights the other types. Compared to the rest of us, Artisans seem to experience the world in a kind of slow motion, unhurried and unconcerned, more sensually absorbed in each moment as it passes. The rest of us rush life, translating experience into language, and complicating the moment with memories and expectations—consciousness, as Hegel said, killing everything it touches. But the Artisans' unique grasp of the moment, detached from the flow of time and held close to the body, nourishes their spontaneity, allowing them an artistry and a split-second agility simply denied most of us, exiled as we are from the immediate world by words and time.

And of all the Artisans, the Sensualists play at life most effortlessly—and most seductively. Indeed, it is very much the Sensualists' freedom from consciousness, their indifference to our intellectual complications—their innocence, really—that makes them so attractive to many of us. This is the Sensualist's typical Pygmalion project: they draw us unconsciously to their carefree way of living, tempting us to abandon our hurry and concern, to give ourselves up to the pleasure of the moment. For most other types, however, such momentary pleasure is just that, short-lived and finally unfulfilling. Loving a Sensualist is a little like taking a wonderful vacation; the carefreeness and spontaneity are great fun for a while, exciting and refreshing, but are eventually frustrating, since the relationship rarely gets beyond the early stage of easy intimacy. When partners of other type attempt to deepen the relationship into serious ritual, personal caring, or intellectual sharing, Sensualists often become edgy and start looking for the door, leaving the partner disappointed, and more often than not feeling a bit betrayed. Marie senses this essential ambivalence in loving the Sensualist after observing Meursault's polite detachment in their discussion of love and marriage:

> Then she said she wondered if she really loved me or not. I, of course, couldn't enlighten her as to that. And, after another silence, she murmured something about my being "a queer fellow." "And I daresay that's why I love you," she added. "But maybe that's why one day I'll come to hate you."
>
> To which I had nothing to say, so I said nothing.[15]

Meursault, much more responsive to foreplay than foresight, declines speculation on such abstract notions as Marie's feelings of love and hate, and remains blankly silent.

Oliver Mellors

This love-hate scenario is played out in one other arena—the bedroom—and the master of this more intimate side of the Sensualist character is, without question, D.H. Lawrence. In *Lady Chatterley's Lover,* his most lucid novel,

---

[15] Albert Camus, *The Stranger,* p. 53.

Lawrence captures both the strength and weakness of the Sensualist lover in Oliver Mellors, Lord Chatterley's gamekeeper. Mellors is the classic Sensualist, reticent, clever with his hands, at home in the deep English woods, a physical, unconscious man, or rather, a man quietly in touch with a concrete center of awareness (called "blood consciousness") that Lawrence believed had been virtually lost in modern industrial life. When Connie Chatterley, a restless "NF" Idealist searching for spiritual peace in the woods, happens upon the gamekeeper at work over his traps, she falls immediately under his sensual spell: Mellors appears

> solitary, and intent, like an animal that works alone....Silently, patiently....It was the stillness, and the timeless sort of patience, in a man impatient and passionate, that touched Connie's womb. She saw it in his bent head, the quick quiet hands, the crouching of his slender, sensitive loins; something patient and withdrawn. She felt his experience had been deeper and wider than her own; much deeper and wider, and perhaps more deadly. And this relieved her of herself; she felt almost irresponsible.
>
> So she sat in the doorway of the hut in a dream, utterly unaware of time.[16]

Mellors' sexual attractiveness is not muscular; as a man he is slender and somewhat frail, but as the male animal he is quietly powerful, absorbed in the moment, perhaps dangerously passionate—although seeing him as "deep" is surely an Idealist's romantic attribution. (Idealists often

---

[16] D.H. Lawrence, *Lady Chatterley's Lover*, p. 83.

invest the Artisan's stillness with profound meaning.) But note also that Mellors' unconscious power is mesmerizing—and liberating: Lady Chatterley, morally bound to her crippled, sexless husband (who consoles himself with the "supreme pleasure of the life of the mind"), feels profoundly drawn out of her repressed, mentalized self by Mellors, relieved of the burden of consciousness.

This psychological release soon turns physical, of course, and the celebrated scenes that follow explore Connie's sexual awakening quite explicitly. In an unconscious Sensualist Pygmalion project, Mellors leads Connie further and further into the flames of sensuality, what Lawrence called "the baptism of fire," and she finds unspeakable contentment in his arms. But all through their relationship, the gamekeeper has difficulty burning out of Connie her nagging Idealist dissatisfaction with the impersonality of their passion. After their first love-making in the woods, for example, Connie hurries home to sort out her feelings:

> What sort of man was he, really? Did he really like her? Not much, she felt. Yet he was kind. There was something, a sort of warm naive kindness, curious and sudden, that almost opened her womb to him. But she felt he might be kind like that to any woman. Though even so, it was curiously soothing, comforting. And he was a passionate man, wholesome and passionate. But perhaps he wasn't quite individual enough; he might be the same with any woman as he had been with her. It really wasn't personal. She was only really a female to him.[17]

---

[17] D.H. Lawrence, *Lady Chatterley's Lover*, p. 113.

Mellors is a wonderful lover, tender and strangely innocent for all his experience, as he begins touching Connie's body into life; but intellectually Connie can't help wanting something more—recognition of her as a person, commitment to her as an individual, some basis of love beyond the faceless joining of male and female.

Mellors' Dionysian call is powerful, however, and part of Connie longs to abandon her Idealist self-consciousness and be taken over by the impersonality of Sensualist passion: "Ah yes," she dreams, "to be passionate like a Baccante, like a Bacchanal fleeing through the woods," with "no independent personality." But though she feels the rapture of "the Bacchae in her limbs and her body," her more nurturing Idealist instincts counsel caution: "but while she felt this, her heart was heavy. She did not want it, it was...barren, birthless." Indeed, in a later scene, even after all her mental resistance has melted away and she has given herself fully, Connie returns to consciousness alone and afraid:

> When awareness of the outside began to come back, she clung to his breast, murmuring: "My love! My love!" And he held her silently. And she curled on his breast, perfect.
>
> But his silence was fathomless. His hands held her like flowers, so still and strange. "Where are you?" she whispered to him. "Where are you? Speak to me! Say something to me!"
>
> He kissed her softly, murmuring: "Ay, my lass!"
>
> But she did not know what he meant, she did not know where he was. In his silence he seemed lost to her.
>
> "You love me, don't you?" she murmured.

> "Ay, tha knows!" he said
> "But tell me!" she pleaded.
> "Ay! Ay! 'asn't ter felt it?" he said dimly, but softly and surely...
> "Say you'll always love me!' she pleaded.
> "Ay!" he said, abstractedly. And she felt her questions driving him away...
> "And will you never leave me?" she said.
> "Dunna ask them things," he said.
> "But you do believe I love you?" she said.
> "Tha loved me just now, wider than iver tha thout tha would. But who knows what'll appen, once tha starts thinkin' about it!"[18]

Like Nick and Marjorie, like Meursault and Marie—like most Sensualists and mates of other type—Mellors and Connie are speaking of love on two very different, perhaps incompatible levels. For all the physical peace Mellors gives her, all the rest from mindfulness, Connie needs love to have a daylight face as well, and so pleads with Mellors to come out of his darkness and silence, to acknowledge her as a person, to say the words of love and to promise the future. Mellors, on the other hand, spent and sleepy, slow to rouse from unconsciousness, answers as if from another world, and in the more intimate Derbyshire dialect he always resorts to in love-making: "Ay," he assures her, she has felt his love, she "knows" his love in her body, timelessly, without words or "thinkin'," and anything more conscious can only drive them from their sensual paradise. Indeed, and paradoxically, Connie's pleas for love themselves break the spell of love, asking Mellors for words he cannot give, and threatening the very security she seeks.

---

[18] D.H. Lawrence, *Lady Chatterley's Lover*, pp. 164-5.

Lawrence clearly believed that the world outside of their timeless, flower-like embrace threatened Connie and Mellors, as the ominous last chapters of *Lady Chatterley's Lover* demonstrate, and his criticism of our modern industrial civilization, bureaucratized, spiritualized and intellectualized, is unrelenting. Lawrence, with his own Idealist longing for wholeness, believed we have to rediscover our body, our unconscious, sexual nature, to bring ourselves again into balance; but I suspect he also knew that few of us can be content for very long with the impersonal sexual relationship he saw as the way to salvation for us all. Humans of other type need more from love than Artisan sensual fulfillment, wonderful and necessary as that may be, and will not easily give up their personal gods of duty, spirit, or intellect to embrace Lawrence's primitive gods of the flesh. Thus conflict and dissatisfaction, psychological as well as sexual, are at the very heart of Lawrence's view of men and women, his Artisan men fighting to maintain their sensual freedom, and his Guardian and Idealist women worrying their men into becoming responsible or spirtual mates. And certainly Lawrence struggled with this battle of wills, this internecine Pygmalion project, in his own psyche, torn between the "life of the body" he so ardently believed in and the "life of the mind" he pursued so prolifically as a writer. As Lawrence himself admitted, fully appreciating the paradox involved, "I'm like Carlyle, who, they say, wrote 50 volumes on the value of silence."[19]

---

[19] Quoted from Lawrence's letter to Ernest Collings, 17 Jan., 1913.

Norman Dewers

As I explained at the outset, for all the Sensualists' need for privacy, they are irresistibly playful creatures, quietly seductive; and so, to end this portrait on a lighter note, I want to introduce Norman Dewers, the mischievous, shaggy—and incorrigibly libidinous—hero of Alan Ayckbourn's brilliant comic trilogy, *The Norman Conquests*.

By day, Norman is an unassuming assistant librarian in London, but such a bookish and mild-mannered occupation is only a mask for his Sensualist excursions. (Indeed, the library is primarily a place for Norman to catch up on his sleep—"Why do you think they have the SILENCE notices?" he explains.) By night, and especially on holiday, Norman is an indefatigable philanderer, "magnetic" and "strangely engaging," to use his own words—or as he describes himself to his brother-in-law Reg:

> A man with my type of temperament should really...get through three women a day without even ruffling his hair. That's what I'm like inside. That's my appetite. That's me. I'm a three a day man.[20]

In many ways, Ayckbourn constructs *The Norman Conquests* around this magical number three: there are three plays set in three different parts of the same country house, the action takes place over a three day weekend

---

[20] Alan Ayckbourn, *The Norman Conquests*, p. 45.

in July, and true to his word Norman either patches up, consummates, or arranges three seductions, though it takes him all three days and considerable ruffling.

Norman's first conquest actually began the previous Christmas, when he and his wife Ruth spent the holiday with her family at "Mother's" house in the country. With Ruth upstairs ill in bed, Norman cheered himself up having a little "festive fun" with Ruth's younger sister, Annie. Sensualists may be reluctant with language, but in action they are irrepressible, as Annie well remembers: "Norman doesn't bother with secret signals at all," she confesses to her sister-in-law Sarah; "It was just wham, thump and there we both were on the rug." Annie is a warm and affectionate Idealist saddled with the thankless job of caring for the bedridden "Mother," living alone with her in their dingy, crumbling old Victorian house. Much like the house, Annie is badly in need of love (and refurbishing), and so, that Christmas, when Norman tells her she's beautiful, tells her he loves her, and promises to run off with her for a weekend when he can arrange it, she decides to play along for awhile, even though, knowing Norman's impulsiveness, she "didn't think it would ever happen." To Annie, the proposed weekend is not much more than a rather guilty fantasy of fresh air and romantic release ("I'm longing to see the sea again. I've forgotten what it looks like"); to Norman, however, in true Sensualist style, the plan is for "a really *dirty* weekend," an "adventure," and an "experience for both of us."

This clandestine weekend is the timeframe for all three plays, as Norman tries his best to keep his adventure from slipping through his fingers. He has booked the hotel (there was a cancellation in East Grinstead), and Annie has called her brother Reg and his wife Sarah down from London to care for "Mother"; but when the fateful Saturday arrives (and each play begins its turn at the events), comical complications immediately ensue. First of all, Annie is conscience-stricken, "feeling sick all morning" thinking about the tryst, and nervously spills the whole embarrassing story to Sarah. Sarah, a wicked caricature of a Guardian (more about her in Volume Two), flurries grimly into action to split up the pair, indeed, to make sure everyone behaves in a civilized manner. On his side, Norman seeks solace with Dionysus, getting "disgustingly drunk" on homemade dandelion wine, phoning up Ruth in London to vent his rage, and terrifying Annie and Sarah by storming upstairs to attack "Mother." Finally, when Ruth drives down Sunday morning to make sense of all the belligerent shouting on the phone, the stage is set for Norman's favorite sort of holiday. Ruth observes that Norman likes to have "three emotions for every occasion," and thus, with three angry women to soothe and win over to his side, Norman is in his glory.

Norman wants to make up with Annie at first opportunity, and so he follows her about with all the woolly innocence of the Old English sheepdog he reminds her of. Finding Annie alone in the dining room Sunday night (putting away the knives and forks), Norman "*creeps in*," as Ayckbourn puts it, and plays for sympathy:

> NORMAN: [*loudly*] Oh Annie, I need you. [*He moves to her.*]

> ANNIE: Ssh. [*She pulls away*] Norman...
> NORMAN: What's wrong?
> ANNIE: Nothing. Just don't...
> NORMAN: Why not? Have you gone off me?
> ANNIE: Well, slightly—no. You know...
> NORMAN: What about me? I mean, us.
> ANNIE: [*sharp*] What about us, Norman?[21]

Norman's untimely slip into the self-serving singular ("What about me") nearly ruins his pose as the wounded, yearning lover, but undismayed he surprises Annie later that night in the sitting room (with the house quiet, and everyone else gone to bed), and adds his famous animal magnetism to his appeal:

> NORMAN: Can I kiss you good night?
> ANNIE: No.
> NORMAN: Can I kiss you goodbye then? Please.
> ANNIE: Norman. You are definitely evil.
> NORMAN: I love you.
> ANNIE: No.
> NORMAN: Kiss?
> ANNIE: Not until you take that back...
> NORMAN: All right. I don't love you. Can I have a kiss, please?[22]

Norman's lost-puppy combination of vulnerability and playfulness quickly melts Annie's resistance (Idealists almost always fall for a paradox); and after he teases her onto their rug, they kiss passionately. Indeed, the next morning before Norman and Ruth leave for London, and after her ponderous local suitor Tom (the "rambling vet") has frustrated her again with his slowness off the

---

[21] Alan Ayckbourn, *The Norman Conquests*, pp. 54-55.

[22] Alan Ayckbourn, *The Norman Conquests*, p. 139.

mark, Annie runs to Norman pleading for another go at their holiday:

> ANNIE: [*a wail*] I want to go to East Grinstead.
> NORMAN: [*soothing her*] All right. Fine. I'll take you. I'll take you.
> ANNIE: [*tearfully*] Will you?
> NORMAN: Just say the word. Come on now, don't cry. I'll make you happy. Don't worry. I'll make you happy.[23]

Pleasure is the Sensualist's first objective in life, and much like Meursault agreeing to marry Marie in *The Stranger,* Norman is perfectly willing—in this case delighted—to share himself with Annie any time she wants.

Norman must also placate his wife over the weekend—after all, Annie is off him much of the time, and Ruth pays most of his bills. And so, after Sarah catches him kissing Annie Sunday night, making such a hysterical scene that Ruth comes downstairs in Norman's dressing gown and orders them all to bed (separate beds), Norman needs all his Sensualist artistry. Ruth is an "NT" Rational whom Norman married, he tells Annie, out of "uncontrollable animal lust," but whom now he accuses of coldness, arrogance, and an almost clinical insensitivity: "if you gave Ruth a rose," Norman grumbles, "she'd peel all the petals off to make sure there weren't any greenfly. And [then] she'd turn around and say, do you call that a rose? Look at it, it's all in bits." On her side, Ruth married Norman for his liveliness and spontaneity, although when he proposed to her (cornering

---

[23] Alan Ayckbourn, *The Norman Conquests,* pp. 87-88.

her in a crowded lift, and enlisting everyone's sympathy) she sensed her mistake: "that was the first time I really felt like throttling Norman." However, Rationals are both loyal and eminently pragmatic in their personal relationships, and once married, Ruth soon learned to tolerate Norman's bizarre emotional gestures, to "keep smiling" and not to take him too seriously:

> It's a bit like owning an oversized unmanageable dog, being married to Norman. He's not very well house-trained, he needs continual exercise...and it's sensible to lock him up if you have visitors...But I'd hate to get rid of him.[24]

Although the "dog" simile is apt, Ruth has no illusions about "owning" Norman, and only her typically Rational disinterest in possessing the spouse[25] keeps them at all compatible: "You couldn't possibly take Norman away from me," she explains in her logical fashion to Annie, since "That assumes I own him in the first place. I've never done that. I always feel with Norman that I have him on loan from somewhere. Like one of his library books."

Still, after the ugly scene with Sarah and Annie on Sunday night, Ruth's patience is at an end, and "simply bloody livid" she berates Norman for his humiliating indiscretion: "You are deceitful, odious, conceited, self-centred, selfish, inconsiderate and shallow." Rationals are embarrassed by such highly charged emotional displays (not to mention such redundancy), and Ruth

---

[24] Alan Ayckbourn, *The Norman Conquests*, p. 195.

[25] David Keirsey and Marilyn Bates, *Please Understand Me*, p. 89.

quickly regains her composure, acknowledging that, after five years of trying, their marriage—and her Pygmalion project—is no longer workable:

> You're obviously not made to be married. You never were. Stupid of me to try and make you behave like a husband in the first place. You'd be much happier if you were perfectly free, flitting from woman to woman as the mood takes you.[26]

Norman's response to such philosophical resignation is, not surprisingly, as lovably deceitful and selfish a seduction as he can manage. Tendering his best "doggie look," Norman denies kissing Annie and insists the whole weekend idea was a gesture of love for Ruth. Ruth holds out at first—"I'm not in the mood for games Norman"—but toughminded Rationals are often surprisingly easy marks for Artisan charm, and she soon surrenders to Norman's familiar appeal: he coaxes her onto the well-worn rug, and as he pulls her down to him he promises, "it's nice on the rug....It can be our rug."

"Familiar" is certainly the word for Norman, and the third female in the family he makes a play for is his sister-in-law Sarah. On the surface of it, Norman and Sarah would seem to have pretty unlikely expectations of romance. She is an indefatigable wife and mother (Ruth calls her "Mother Doom")—a prim and proper Guardian much too busy inspecting the silver and rationing the wine to worry about being "happy" in Norman's sense of the word. Indeed, she barely finds time to

---

[26] Alan Ayckbourn, *The Norman Conquests*, p. 143.

come and help Annie have her holiday: "It was difficult enough this weekend," she tells Norman; "I was racing around organizing things, arranging." And Sarah especially resents Norman's cavalier husbandly attitude: she admits to Annie, "I would not wish my worst enemy married to a man like [that]," and when Norman begins flirting with Sarah herself ("I'm very warm and affectionate, you know"), she cuts him dead: "Yes. So are dogs. But they don't make particularly good husbands." At the same time, Norman finds Sarah's complaining and meddling almost insufferable: he describes her as a "cow elephant" trampling over her husband Reg, and he likens his own, less frequent contacts with her to a case of "athlete's foot. You make me irritable."

On this magical weekend, however, Norman is game even for Sarah: "This boy can do no wrong," he crows; "He has the midas touch. Every woman turns to gold." And thus, despite their almost instinctive antipathy, when alone with Sarah in the garden on his drunken Saturday night, Norman reaches out unsteadily and touches her hand:

> SARAH: [*without moving her hand away*] Oh, Norman. Ruth, then Annie, then me. Be your age.
> NORMAN: [*taking her hand more firmly*] I don't mean any harm...
> SARAH: You're so dopey, I don't know how anybody could fall for you.
> NORMAN: God knows. [*He kisses her hand*] Animal magnetism.
> SARAH: You've no morals. No nothing, have you?

> NORMAN: I'm full of love.
> SARAH: And wine...
> NORMAN: [*moving closer*] By God, you're lovely.[27]

Although Sarah's tone is properly sober and disapproving, she is hardly immune to Norman's Dionysian call, and indeed she finds herself kissing him madly before she remembers herself and lurches away, insisting frantically (hoping to reestablish their conventional roles), "I want to get you something to eat. I want you to eat something...please let me get you something to eat." As we know, however, Norman's appetite is hard to satisfy, and thus on Monday morning, after the most "shattering weekend" in Sarah's memory, he approaches her again, offering this time to cheer her up with (you guessed it) a friendly holiday at the sea:

> NORMAN: ...I'd like to see you happy, Sarah.
> SARAH: Yes?
> NORMAN: Yes. Is that wrong of me? To want to see you happy?
> SARAH: Depends on how you do it.
> NORMAN: I'd give you a good time. We'd have fun. Have you ever been to Bournemouth? It's a great place. Laugh a minute.
> SARAH: I can just see us going.
> NORMAN: I'd very much like to make you happy.[28]

Norman's Sensualist generosity seems so heartfelt and boundless ("I want to make everyone happy," he declares

---

[27] Alan Ayckbourn, *The Norman Conquests*, p. 186.

[28] Alan Ayckbourn, *The Norman Conquests*, p. 81.

roundly; "It's my mission in life") that Sarah again gratefully forgets her normal responsibilities and inhibitions, and as if "giddy" with wine herself, dreams of her own "nice dirty weekend" free of Reg and the children. She smiles knowingly, suggests Norman ring her up when Reg is away, and happily *"grunts,"* as Ayckbourne puts it, with furtive anticipation.

In truth, Norman attempts a fourth rendezvous (of sorts) this weekend, and though only a wild, drunken gesture, it puts the finishing touches on my portrait of the Sensualist. After Sarah escapes Norman's clutches Saturday night in the garden, Reg comes out with another bottle of wine, and he and Norman drink under the stars. Norman swigs from the bottle—"I'm all man tonight"—and gets more and more in touch with his Sensualist nature:

> It's on such a night as this that all the old base instincts of primitive man, the hunter, come flooding up. You long to be away—free—filled with the urge to rape and pillage and conquer.[29]

Reg seems more concerned with his varicose veins than with any strenuous-sounding "lust for conquest," but Norman proceeds to slur out his suddenly inspired vision of a holiday just for the men:

> NORMAN: Well, in a way—no not a holiday—that sounds so damn conventional. I want us just to go.... And see things. And taste things.

---

[29] Alan Ayckbourn, *The Norman Conquests*, p. 191.

> And smell things. And touch things....touch trees—and grass—and—earth. Let's touch earth together, Reg.
> REG: Where were you thinking of going?
> NORMAN: Everywhere. Let's see everywhere. Let's be able to say—we have seen and experienced everything.[30]

Reg doesn't know quite what to make of Norman's unexpected affection—"[...*embracing Reg*] Oh Reg... You're my brother, Reg....I love you, Reg"—but Norman's instinctive (and inebriated) longing to return to a manly life of the senses brings us full circle, back to the earthy Sensualists of Hemingway, Camus, and Lawrence. Norman may be a somewhat puny and lecherous version of Oliver Mellors, but his nature—as gamesman and as lover—is just as robust: as Norman laments himself (with a few word-changes for clarity),

> The trouble is, I was born in the wrong damn fiction. Look at me. A Sensualist trapped in a witty domestic comedy. The tragedy of my life, Norman Dewers—Sensualist and assistant librarian.[31]

* * * * *

Sensualists, to summarize, may appear detached and self-contained in their private moments, but in their sexual relationships their more engaging nature comes

---

[30] Alan Ayckbourn, *The Norman Conquests*, p. 192.

[31] Alan Ayckbourn, *The Norman Conquests*, p. 45. The real speech reads: "The trouble is, I was born in the wrong damn body. Look at me. A gigolo trapped in a haystack. The tragedy of my life, Norman Dewers—gigolo and assistant librarian."

into play, and is nearly impossible to refuse. In this sense Keirsey is right when he refers to the Sensualists as "Composers": they call to the other types with a siren song, seducing us with their kindness and their infectious spontaneity—composing us to their own style with their intimate artistry. Their only tactic, really, is their irresistible hedonism, and their Pygmalion projects, while not entirely incidental, are the most benign and pleasurable of all. In loving a Sensualist, our wisest course is not to take them too seriously nor to demand too much conscious devotion from them, but simply to enjoy them as incomparable lovers, letting them charm us for a while into their sensuous world.

Chapter 3
The Performer

GUILDENSTERN: Well, aren't you going to change into your costume?
PLAYER: I never change out of it, sir.

—Tom Stoppard[1]

As the preceding chapter's noticeably masculine cast may suggest, Sensualist women are hard to come by in literature. Both the "strong, silent type" and the playfully seductive "Casanova" tend to be male ideals, and of the few female Sensualists who come to mind, most are hopelessly romanticized by their male authors. Justine Hosnani, a Sensualist in Lawrence Durrell's *Alexandria Quartet*, for example, is given almost mythical proportions in her dark sexuality: "Like all amoral people," one character insists, "she verges on the Goddess."[2] And Vladimir Nabokov's pedophiliac narrator in *Lolita* knows full well that "What I had possessed was not she, but my own creation, another, fanciful Lolita."[3] However, for

[1] Tom Stoppard, *Rosencrantz & Guildenstern Are Dead*, p. 33.

[2] Lawrence Durrell, *Justine*, p. 77.

[3] Vladimir Nabokov, *Lolita*, p. 64.

the *extraverted* Players (whom Myers called the "ESFP"s), the story is quite different. The female extraverted Player—the party girl, the showgirl, the "good time" girl—is a well-known character in fiction and film, though all too often degraded into the "dumb blond" or good-hearted whore. Keirsey calls the extraverted Players, male and female, the "Performers"[4] to capture their almost incessant need to be on stage, entertaining those around them, though again, sadly, this "more the merrier" exuberance is often judged in women to be wantonness and exhibitionism.

Sally Bowles

One female Performer who overcomes such stereotypes is Sally Bowles, the audacious, free-spirited nightclub singer in Christopher Isherwood's *The Berlin Stories*, familiarized as the Liza Minnelli character in Bob Fosse's stunning film, *Cabaret*. Sally is a born Performer, though certainly not a gifted one. She is in fact a terrible singer, but after watching her at the cheap, arty barroom where she works, Isherwood concedes that "her performance was, in its own way, effective" because of the utter audacity of her character: she stands on the platform, at her ease, with an "air of not caring a curse what people thought of her,...arms hanging carelessly limp, and a take-it-or-leave-it grin on her face."[5] Sally goes on stage

[4] David Keirsey, *Portraits of Temperament*, p. 40; also referred to as "Entertainers" in *Please Understand Me.*

[5] Christopher Isherwood, *Goodbye To Berlin*, p. 25.

for the applause, of course—she loves the attention, the verification of her social impact. But Performers are typically carefree and confident of their impulses, and thus need much less appreciation from the audience than most of us. Indeed, above all else, Sally sings for the almost addictive exhilaration of performing. If Sensualist hunters love the danger of stalking their prey alone in the forest, the more gregarious Performers thrill to the heart-stopping adventure of capturing the spotlight, of conquering the moment—the sheer excitement of knocking their audience "dead," as entertainers often put it. This is the Performers' unique way: putting on a show for the fun of it, the immediate sensual impact, and needing little but their own pleasure in return.

Not all Performers are cabaret singers, of course, but even off the stage they entertain us with their flare for living. Sally's private life, for example, is just as much a performance as her nightclub act, a series of outrageous poses designed, with innate artistry, to impress or to scandalize, to excite or to seduce, to delight or to disturb others—to have some sort of dramatic impact on those around her. She dresses the part, in vamp-like black silk and a cape, sometimes adding a white collar, for a "theatrically chaste effect," and accenting her boldness with green fingernails, a dead-white powdered face, and darkly arched eyebrows. She also plays the part, puckering and pouting, incessantly flourishing her "ugly" hands, flattering her friends with breathless affectation ("How marvellous!"), and teasing them with "a silvery little stage-laugh." She even makes up the part as she goes along, time and again smoothing her way by telling "really startling lies, which," Isherwood adds, "she obviously for the moment half-believed."

However, for all her ostentation, Sally is no exhibitionist in desperate need of attention. Isherwood's portrait of the Performer is remarkably restrained in that he attributes no underlying pathological motives to Sally's ceaseless performing. Isherwood seems to understand that Performers are at once affected and natural, artful and artless, instinctively artful, if you will. Sally preens and flirts and dances around the truth not from some nervous compulsion, but spontaneously, from her seemingly boundless joy of living, and Isherwood happily gives her the spotlight.

Sally makes love with the same flourish, constantly seducing some new lover, or being seduced herself. "That's the man I slept with last night," she announces brightly, "he makes love marvelously"; some other "old swine" she is seeing wants her to be his mistress; and she is afraid one younger man will "seduce me down the telephone. He's most terribly passionate." A few pages later she even tries to provoke the intellectual (and homosexual) Isherwood with a similar disclosure: "I didn't sleep a wink last night. I've got a marvelous new lover." But again, Sally is no nymphomaniac hungrily compensating for lack of love. She is naturally promiscuous, taking lovers, much like her singing at the club, simply for the excitement of it, the sensual variety. Though she boasts a good deal about finding a rich lover, as a Performer she is not really calculating enough to be a kept woman: "For a would-be demi-mondaine," Isherwood observes, "she seemed to have surprisingly little business sense." Despite her experience of the world, Sally has a thoroughly disarming innocence about her. She falls in love suddenly, impulsively, absolutely certain each time that she's found the love of her life. Sally may like to dramatize herself as a hardened "old whore," but in fact she wears her heart on her sleeve, loving with the exuberance and the unsophistication of, in Isherwood's phrase, a "naughty child...amusing the grown-ups."

Sally's Performer style of loving is beautifully detailed in her whirlwind affair with Klaus Linke, her former piano accompanist at the nightclub. An Instrumentalist Artisan himself, Klaus had adored Sally from first sight (as he assures her) but had kept quietly in the background. When they meet at a New Year's Eve party, however, Sally immediately falls head over heels—or believes she has, as she runs to tell Isherwood the next morning:

> I gave her [a cigarette] and lit the match. She blew out a long cloud of smoke and walked slowly to the window:
>
> "I'm most terribly in love with him."
>
> She turned, frowning slightly; crossed to the sofa and curled herself up carefully, arranging her hands and feet: "At least I think I am," she added.[6]

Sally's performance here is subtle, again artful and artless. Her last comment is not so much cautious as it is

---

[6] Christopher Isherwood, *Goodbye to Berlin*, p. 37.

honestly superficial; she falls in love so frequently and so casually that she's not quite sure what the real thing feels like, though she's "certain" this is it. At the same time, a certain staginess or melodrama veils the whole scene. She wants to believe (and she wants Isherwood to believe) that she is a woman of grand passion, and that she has found a love deep and everlasting, different from all the others; and so, always the Performer, Sally plays the serious lover searching her heart, though the sincerity of her words is as carefully arranged as her pose on the sofa.

The affair flourishes, Sally is with Klaus day and night for two weeks, and for all her pretended introspection the love is clearly Dionysian. Klaus is "so marvelously primitive: just like a faun," Sally tells Isherwood, and she herself feels "like a most marvellous nymph, or something, miles away from anywhere, in the middle of a forest." Artisan love is at times precarious, however, and true to type Klaus suddenly leaves for a job in England, soothing Sally with slick endearments, but finally writing her the familiar apology: "I see now...that I behaved very selfishly. I thought only of my own pleasure." Sally's response to such a rude jilting is a complete cycle of attitudes, each in turn shedding light on the Performer's nature.

First of all, Performers — ebullient and optimistic — typically refuse to recognize their problems, preferring to believe that everything's fine and for the best. And thus Sally, ignoring the darker side, trying to be brave, first plays at self-sacrifice (feeling "all marvelous and ethereal"):

> I don't suppose I shall ever marry him. It would ruin our careers. You see, Christopher...it wouldn't be good for him to always have me hanging about.[7]

Facing the truth comes next, and soon Sally's magnanimity turns to wistful self-evaluation. She describes herself with surprisingly profound understanding, perhaps even voicing the innermost fear of all Performer women, though I suspect the insight is more Isherwood's than her own:

> But seriously, I believe I'm a sort of Ideal Woman, if you know what I mean. I'm the sort of woman who can take men away from their wives, but I could never keep anybody for long. And that's because I'm the type which every man imagines he wants, until he gets me; then he finds he doesn't really, after all.[8]

Eventually, as the galling truth of Klaus's leaving sinks in, Sally's wise sadness changes to anger and cynicism. Klaus becomes "that swine," and her idea of love becomes coldly practical, a simple matter of money: "if only I could get a really rich man as my lover," she schemes; "I'd do anything, just now, to get rich." Attuned as they are to concrete reality, Artisans are naturally cynical and

---

[7] Christopher Isherwood, *Goodbye to Berlin*, p. 39.

[8] Christopher Isherwood, *Goodbye to Berlin*, p. 50.

hard to disillusion; and though Sally (as a warm-hearted Performer) is more easily seduced by theatrics than the other Artisans, when she does finally see that the performance is over, she bitterly resents having played the fool. However, Performers are never down for long, and Sally finally comes full circle to her usual optimism: she vows never to fall in love again, she dedicates herself to her acting (expecting her big break any day), and she pushes herself to re-energize: "Let's go out this evening, Chris. I'm sick of this room. Let's go out and see some life!"

Sally is bitten again in *The Berlin Stories*—as a Performer she is too vivacious and too easily seduced to remain calloused and detached for long. She tries gold-digging a rich American playboy, but she can't keep her feelings out of the arrangement, and as soon as she begins to "adore him" and make wedding plans, he (a Promoter Artisan) flees Berlin with barely a note: "I can't stick this darned town any longer, so am off." And later she becomes engaged to another young con-man after "the most marvellous dinner" and one night in a cheap hotel. When he absconds the next morning with her money, the police question Sally's judgment:

> "You mean to tell me that you became engaged to this man when you'd only known him a single afternoon?"
>
> "Certainly."
>
> "Isn't that, well—rather unusual?"
>
> "I suppose it is," Sally seriously agreed. "But nowadays, you know, a girl can't afford to keep a man waiting."[9]

[9] Christopher Isherwood, *Goodbye to Berlin*, p. 73.

Sally's answer, like much of her life, is improvised, a Performer's ad-libbed defense of her own impulsiveness. She was not desperate to marry, just in a hurry—nothing unusual for a Performer. Indeed, Sally is impulsive to the end, vanishing from Berlin, and out of Isherwood's life forever, promising to "write properly," but managing only two scribbled postcards, and then a silence such as falls when the party is over.

Brett Ashley

I don't want to leave the impression that all female Performers are as frivolous or as out of control as Sally Bowles. Throughout her adventures in *The Berlin Stories* Sally is just nineteen years old, and she plays her outrageous role perhaps too eagerly: "Do I shock you when I talk like that, Christopher darling?" A more mature, and certainly more knowing female Performer is Hemingway's Lady Brett Ashley in *The Sun Also Rises*.

Much as Sally scandalizes 1930 Berlin, Brett sets her own, defiant fashion in Paris between the wars, wearing her hair "brushed back like a boy's," and "a man's felt hat" pulled down to one side. She almost always plays to an audience, bar-hopping with "a crowd of young men" in the Bohemian Quarter, and regarding quiet drinks and private conversations as a terrible bore: "You and your quiet," Brett complains to one admirer, "What is it men feel about quiet?" "We like it," he explains, "like you like noise, my dear." She is charming and witty ("I always joke people"), and she lies her way out of difficult spots with a crinkle of her eye and a practised laugh. Though not a professional entertainer like Sally, Brett is a natural Performer, poised in the spotlight, in one scene becoming very nearly a goddess of Artisan festivity. In Pamplona for the Fiesta, a week-long orgy of drinking and street dancing, Brett is swept up by the crowd as an idol:

> Some dancers formed a circle around Brett and started to dance...They were all chanting. Brett wanted to dance but they did not want her to. They wanted her as an image to dance around.[10]

Hemingway depicts the famous Fiesta in the novel as truly a Performer's paradise—"the dancing went on, the drinking kept up, the noise went on...and it seemed as though nothing could have any consequences"—and Brett, amused and excited, "seated on a wine-cask," reigns playfully over the Dionysian celebration.

Also like Sally, Brett seduces men effortlessly and impulsively. When Robert Cohn, a fatuously romantic, second-rate writer (the kind Hemingway often ridiculed), begins following Brett around, she avoids him for a while, but then steals off to San Sebastian with him for two weeks before her fiancé arrives in Paris. The affair is insignificant for Brett, a sudden, kindly gesture to help loosen the young writer up—"I rather thought it would be good for him"—and is over just as suddenly, Cohn proving "a little dull" on further acquaintance. Making love is just good entertainment for Brett, she means no

---

[10] Ernest Hemingway, *The Sun Also Rises*, p. 155.

harm, and later, when Cohn's injured pride turns to belligerence (he calls Brett a "Circe," claiming "she turns men into swine"), she sympathizes with his old-fashioned ideas about love: "I do know how he feels," she confesses, "He can't believe it didn't mean anything."

At the same time, Brett is also easily infatuated herself. When she first sees Pedro Romero, the brilliant young Sensualist bullfighter, she can't keep her eyes off his tight green trousers; and soon, desperately in love with Romero (without ever having spoken to him), she begs for advice and assistance from Jake Barnes, her faithful confidant:

> "I'm a goner. I'm mad about the Romero boy. I'm in love with him, I think."
> "I wouldn't be if I were you."
> "I can't help it. I'm a goner. It's tearing me all up inside."
> "Don't do it."
> "I can't help it. I've never been able to help anything."
> "You ought to stop it."
> "How can I stop it? I can't stop things....I've got to do something. I've got to do something I really want to do....I've always done just what I wanted."[11]

Brett's overpowering urge to act on her sexual impulse, to "do something" about her desire for Romero, is absolutely characteristic of the Performer (most Artisans for that matter), and is at the very heart of their passion

---

[11] Ernest Hemingway, *The Sun Also Rises*, pp. 183-184.

for seduction. Some Performers, of course, control this desire by flirting with the opposite sex, though they are likely to do so openly and thoughtlessly, embarrassing their spouses or loved ones. For many Performers, however, to wait, to consider, to restrain—to "help it" somehow—is nearly impossible. The pressure to act builds painfully, like a dam swelling to burst, and their only release is to yield to their compulsion. Indeed, after Jake reluctantly agrees to introduce them, Brett works her spell on Romero and ends up becoming his mistress, though she feels like "such a bitch" for her shamelessness.

However, for all her Performer's impulsiveness, Brett is a more complex character than Sally Bowles, or at least older and more self-aware. Brett is almost twice Sally's age, she has twice married men "she didn't love," and she has lived through the devastation of World War I. In her sobering experience of life, she has come to understand that our actions have consequences, that, as she tells Jake, "we pay for everything we do." This idea—startling to an Artisan—that our actions are not totally free, that eventually life presents a bill, is a major theme in *The Sun Also Rises,* and throughout Hemingway's fiction. Indeed, Hemingway's great subject (from the point-of-view of temperament theory, at least) is the free-living, irresponsible Artisan learning to accept a primitive sense of responsibility, acceding to a rudimentary moral code. Facing life squarely as it is, paying the bill for our actions without complaint, refusing to coerce for personal advantage (in essence, no Pygmalion projects): Hemingway's stories often turn on such points of integrity, courage, and personal honor. His heroes struggle to live by this rugged code, even as they face death; while his other characters, those who (like Robert Cohn) want to appear heroic without paying the price—who want something for nothing—bear the brunt of Hemingway's scorn. In Brett's case, she has learned, painfully and barely, to look at life without illusions, and to stifle her desire when the price is too high, or when it can't be paid at all.

Brett's hardest lesson in disillusionment, certainly, grows out of her love for Jake Barnes. Jake is the man Brett cares for most deeply in the novel, a wounded Sensualist who could satisfy her completely, if only he were whole. However, Jake was castrated in the war, and—beyond his sexual impotence—his maiming has left him emotionally scarred, psychologically lost, even haunted at night (Jake is as close as Hemingway ever came to a soul-searching Idealist narrator). And in his stolen moments alone with Brett, Jake strains against his fate: "Couldn't we live together, Brett? Couldn't we just live together?" Though Brett loves Jake helplessly and cannot bear to be separated from him for long, she knows her Performer's nature too well to indulge the impulse:

> "I don't think so. I'd just *tromper* [deceive] you with everybody. You couldn't stand it."
> "I stand it now."
> "That would be different. It's my fault, Jake. It's the way I'm made."
> "Couldn't we go off in the country for a while?"

> "It wouldn't be any good. I'll go if you like. But I couldn't live quietly in the country. Not with my own true love."[12]

Brett's closing line gently mocks Jake's sentimentality, the tender irony revealing a terrible sense of loss. Though an escape to the country sounds idyllic (a kind of "separate peace" as in *A Farewell to Arms*), Brett knows she cannot live a fairy tale, and refuses "to go through that hell again" of a quiet life together. Their only recourse is to face the truth honestly, to give up any hopeless Pygmalion dreams, and to accept the terrible price of having fallen in love in the first place. "When I think of the hell I've put chaps through," Brett concedes, "I'm paying for it all now."

Brett also knows, perhaps because of her love for Jake, that her affair with Romero has its darker consequences. By taking the young Sensualist away from his people and his art, by acting the Pygmalion and "turning his head," Brett can ruin him, corrupt his unconscious virtuosity, turn him from a graceful, powerful artist into an obedient, emasculated showman like many of the other matadors after the war. And thus, in spite of her passion for the boy, she realizes she must act bravely and give him up, as she tearfully relates to Jake:

> "I made him go."
> "Why didn't you keep him?"
> "I don't know. It isn't the sort of thing one does. I don't think I hurt him any....He shouldn't be living with any one. I realized

---

[12] Ernest Hemingway, *The Sun Also Rises*, p. 55.

> that right away....You know I'd have lived with him if I hadn't seen it was bad for him....I'm not going to be one of those bitches that ruins children."[13]

Acting against impulse doesn't come easily for a Performer, however, and Brett trembles and sobs all through her story, trying repeatedly to evade the conflict: "let's not talk about it. Let's never talk about it." On the brighter side, she's proud of her sacrifice: "You know I feel rather damned good, Jake." She will be optimistic; she may be torn up now, things may be dark, but the sun also rises, and tomorrow will solve her problems. Honoring the Hemingway code is ambivalent consolation for Brett, but as a Performer she will be cheerful and put on her best face. "You know it makes one feel rather good deciding not to be a bitch," Brett concludes, voicing the minimal morality of Hemingway's Artisan world: "It's sort of what we have instead of God."

Walter Morel

Performers may prefer to avoid serious relationships, either out of playfulness or practical morality, but when emotionally committed they can become tenacious

---

[13] Ernest Hemingway, *The Sun Also Rises*, pp. 241-243. Note also that Romero wants to marry Brett and to feminize *her*: "He really wanted to marry me. So I couldn't go away from him....After I'd gotten more womanly, of course" (p. 242). Whether this prospect of a traditional marriage—and an incipient Pygmalion project on Romero's part—helps Brett make up her mind to leave Romero is not clear in the novel, but her decision may not be altogether selfless.

Pygmalions. Indeed, I want to turn now to a more troubled relationship, a twisted Artisan-Guardian marriage, and the desperate interpersonal coercion that issues from it.

Walter Morel, the father in D.H. Lawrence's early masterpiece, *Sons and Lovers*, begins the novel a handsome young coal miner, cutting a dazzling figure as he dances at the Erewash Valley Christmas party:

> He was well set-up, erect, and very smart. He had wavy black hair that shone again, and a vigorous black beard that had never been shaved. His cheeks were ruddy, and his red, moist mouth was noticeable because he laughed so often and so heartily. He had that rare thing, a rich, ringing laugh....He was so full of colour and animation, his voice ran so easily into the comic grotesque, he was so ready and so pleasant with everybody....soft, non-intellectual, warm, a kind of gambolling....He danced well, as if it were natural and joyous in him to dance...a certain subtle exultation like glamour in his movement, and his face the flower of his body, ruddy, with tumbled black hair, and laughing alike whatever partner he bowed above.[14]

Morel is the archetypal male Performer, exuberant, boisterous, naturally cocky and graceful, literally glistening in the spotlight of others' attention. He weaves his way effortlessly through the party, pausing here and there to

---

[14] D.H. Lawrence, *Sons and Lovers*, p. 9.

tease or to dance, playing with each moment as it comes, and warming each guest in turn with his healthy sexuality. To the men he is a "jolly" drinking buddy; to the women, particularly the Guardian women, he is curiously attractive.

And indeed, as Gertrude Coppard, a "high-minded, and really stern" young Guardian, sits alone and watches him weave his spell at the party, she is fascinated by his warmth and spontaneity, and envious of his unconscious sexuality:

> the dusky, golden softness of this man's sensuous flame of life, that flowed off his flesh like the flame from a candle, not baffled and gripped into incandescence by thought and spirit as her life was, seemed to her something wonderful, beyond her.[15]

As surely as Connie Chatterley fell under Mellors's wordless spell in the woods, Gertrude for the first time in her life feels the intoxication of Dionysian revelry when Morel approaches her for a dance: "A warmth radiated through her" when the miner smiles on her, "as if she had drunk wine." This is the power of the Performers, whether entertaining an audience, or simply amusing loved ones in relationships: they free us from ourselves, lifting us beyond our cares and hurries, charming us for a little while into their more sensual, spontaneous world.

---

[15] D.H. Lawrence, *Sons and Lovers*, p. 10.

On his side, Morel is also curiously drawn to Gertrude. Her sober, superior manner is surprisingly heady wine for the young man:

> Walter Morel seemed melted away before her. She was to the miner that thing of mystery and fascination, a lady.[16]

When Gertrude keeps her head and refuses to dance (she is "rather contemptuous of dancing"), Morel seems genuinely impressed, almost delighted, with her strict disapproval: he happily apologizes for his lower instincts, "I'm like a pig's tail, I curl because I canna help it," and he compliments her rigidity—"Tha'rt not long in taking the curl out of me." In this scene and many others throughout his fiction, Lawrence seemed to understand intuitively the attraction of opposites that forms the basis of so many of our closest relationships, and that leads to Pygmalion projects. Morel, the free, irresponsible Performer, dancing and flirting with all the girls, for some reason settles reverentially next to Gertrude, his opposite, a severe, reproachful Guardian. Perhaps he's merely challenged by a different kind of female, one not so easily swept off her feet. And yet Morel seems to have a larger interest in Gertrude, as though he senses some quite different cast of personality is needed in his life, someone educated and religious to balance his physical confidence, someone careful and serious to offset his impulsiveness, a clean, sensible woman to rise to from the dark, dirty pits of the mine. Morel, let me be clear, is

---

[16] D.H. Lawrence, *Sons and Lovers*, p. 9.

not in the least discontented with himself or his life. Artisans are rarely self-critical, usually managing to blame others for their insufficiencies. He is simply, and quite impulsively, enamored with the sense of stability, completeness, perhaps even an artistic sense of harmony or counterpoint, that Gertrude would bring him.

Morel soon wins Gertrude's hand by promising with great flourish to reform his wild Performer's ways: no more dancing, even though he had run "quite a famous" (i.e. "scandalous") dancing class for years in the valley; and no more drinking—"He had signed the pledge, and wore the blue ribbon of a teetotaller: he was nothing if not showy." He refurnishes his house to please Gertrude, "with solid, worthy stuff that suited her honest soul," and he promises to return home faithfully after his shift, giving up his usual "stoppin'" to drink with his buddies from the mine. For three months Walter and Gertrude are perfectly happy, wrapped in intimacy, involved more in "love talk" than Pygmalion projects. But at six months the honeymoon abruptly ends. Gertrude discovers, quite by accident, that Morel has let the bill for the furniture go unpaid, simply ignored it; and she learns that their house and the one next door are not his own property, as he had boasted to her. She begins to question Morel about money, making veiled accusations about his honesty; Morel responds sullenly and soon resumes his habit of drinking late on his way home, telling Gertrude he's working overtime at the mine. After confronting his lies, his broken promises, and braving several other "flashes of fear" concerning his Artisan nature, the young wife's

Guardian heart hardens with indignation as she realizes Morel's essential irresponsibility:

> He had begun to neglect her; the novelty of his own home was gone. He had no grit, she said bitterly to herself. What he felt just at the minute, that was all to him. He could not abide by anything. There was nothing at the back of all his show.[17]

Performers quite frequently disillusion their partners, at least to some extent. They can rarely live up to their own pretensions, nor can they sustain for very long their partners' usually romanticized image of their character. The mask eventually slips, and the more noble and sincere the pose—or the attribution—the more bitter the disappointment.

Still, Lawrence describes Walter and Gertrude's months of estrangement with amazing objectivity. Lawrence conceded that *Sons and Lovers* was an autobiographical novel, written at least in part to work out his ambivalent feelings for his own parents. Lawrence, a sickly child, hated his father's coarse and brutal ways, and drew abnormally close to his embattled mother; and yet at this point in the novel Lawrence manages to see fault on both sides. While he obviously sympathizes with Gertrude's disappointment in Morel, he also knew first hand (and deeply resented) the emasculation that such a domineering woman can inflict on the men in her life—sons

---

[17] D.H. Lawrence, *Sons and Lovers*, p. 14.

or lovers. And while clearly Lawrence criticizes Morel's shallowness and irresponsibility, he also admired throughout his fiction men of such "purely sensuous" nature. Here again is the paradox that infuses so much of Lawrence's thought: how to reconcile the mental/spiritual with the physical, how to marry—and keep married—the Guardian or Idealist woman and the Artisan man.

Indeed, in his own way, Morel has tried to be the responsible husband Gertrude wanted, his tail permanently straightened; and he thinks nothing of the lies he has told her—they were necessary to keep her happy, he believes, innocent stories really, hardly lies at all. Unlike their reticent Sensualist brothers, Performers are quite facile with language, but they speak with little conscience, words coming easily and quickly to them, but carrying only momentary conviction. Words are simply a means to an end, and thus, naively, without conscious calculation, Performers will say almost anything to get their way or to smooth a difficult moment, making a wonderful show of compliance or sincerity, but rarely thinking of the moral consequences of their words. (Perhaps this is why Performers make such superb dramatic actors: they can deliver any speech with utter assurance.) To Gertrude, however, locked in her moral outrage, Morel is a fraud and a profoundly weak and sinful man. The puritan in her, humiliated and disappointed (with him, of course, but also with herself for having been such a fool), can no longer forgive her husband for being the playful young peacock she had fallen in love with.

"Something in her proud, honourable soul had crystallised out hard as rock," and she turns on Morel with a dogged resentment.

The "bloody battle" that ensues in *Sons and Lovers* escalates into two reciprocating Pygmalion projects. Gertrude's, the more elaborate, I will discuss in Volume Two, in my portrait of the "ISTJ" Inspector Guardian. Morel's relatively crude and less successful project, however, is at once more straightforward and more self-destructive. Very simply, he begins to bully his wife, and to drink his revenge.

Morel had found Gertrude attractive, in the first place, for her aristocratic manner: she was a "lady" to him, refined and intellectual, someone it thrilled him to set above himself and worship. But as Morel's fancied devotion weakens, and his more earthy, self-centered nature feels his wife's criticism, he finds himself despising Gertrude's superior air, and he sets about breaking her down to his level, "asserting the rights of men and husbands." Morel, once joyous and free, assumes an attitude of "bullying indifference" to Gertrude's tongue lashings, and he even resorts to physical force to compel the respect she denies him for his Artisan ways. He pushes her out of the house one night, bolting the door behind her, as if to say, "I don't care who you are nor what you are, I *shall* have my own way." And he threatens her with violence, and eventually bloodies her brow, insisting that she serve him:

> "Tha should get up, like other women have to, an' wait on a man."

> "Wait on you—wait on you?" she cried. "Yes, I see myself."
> "Yis, an' I'll learn thee tha's got to. Wait on *me*, yes tha sh'lt wait on me—"
> "Never, milord. I'd wait on a dog at the door first."[18]

Morel's rough coercion is a simple, but inevitable response to Gertrude's stinging sarcasm. As a Performer male, Morel has always prided himself on his brash command: he is the cock of the walk, strutting in the spotlight, literally waited on by all the females. Gertrude herself was seduced by this exciting showmanship, but now her mocking deprives him of this masculine arrogance, his "manhood," to use Lawrence's term. Little wonder that Morel's first means of retaliation is to assert his physical strength.

Morel has another, more oblique tactic, however: he turns to heavy drinking. On one level, Morel drinks merely to escape the poisoned atmosphere in his house. After a crushing bout with Gertrude, for example, he typically slips away to the nearest pub, where the drinking and the male company revive his genial Performer spirits: "In a minute or two they had thawed all responsibility out of him, all shame, all trouble, and he was clear as a bell for a jolly night." Performers, as I have said, are experts at shifting blame, and on such a night Morel drinks with Dionysus, for the fraternity and for the release, and what little guilt he feels for bullying his wife vanishes with the pints of beer. But Lawrence understood

---

[18] D.H. Lawrence, *Sons and Lovers*, pp. 38-39.

there was a darker side, and he shows clearly that Morel's drinking is also his way of punishing Gertrude (and controlling her as well) by abusing himself. Morel knows that Gertrude despises him most, and is most humiliated and degraded, when he comes home drunk; and so, "taking his revenge," as Lawrence puts it, Morel drinks himself stupid, mortifying Gertrude at every opportunity. He will make Gertrude sorry—"I'll ma'e yer pay for this"—even by hurting himself; and he will make his wife attend him, even by provoking her scorn.

Let me stress that both Morel's methods of asserting his manhood—physical violence and drunkenness—are, for him, self-defeating. He is no contentious Operator Artisan, rising gladly to the combat in his marriage or capable of enjoying his revenge. He is a more congenial Player, and indeed, his attempts to hurt Gertrude into submission recoil on him terribly, leaving him profoundly wounded. He might bluster and threaten, drink and carouse,

> Yet there was a slight shrinking, a diminishing in his assurance. Physically even, he shrank, and his fine full presence waned. He never grew in the least stout, so that, as he sank from his erect assertive bearing, his physique seemed to contract along with his pride and moral strength.[19]

Certainly not all male Performers resort to such violent or such debilitating tactics in their relationships. Performers would rather hide from trouble, and then escape

[19] D.H. Lawrence, *Sons and Lovers*, p. 26.

before the battle for control becomes too deadly. But trapped in the wrong relationship, committed to the struggle by some stubborn, misdirected desire, the Performer's predisposition is toward manipulative self-destruction.[20] In Walter and Gertrude's marriage, the battle-grip and the victor are clearly defined: "There was this deadlock of passion between them," Lawrence explains, "and she was stronger."

By their third child, then, Morel is a rather pathetic figure, a boorish, posturing Performer trying to match wits—and Pygmalion projects—with an arch and relentless Guardian, yet only wasting his potency, and slowly making way for his sons to become the center of his wife's existence, as well as the focus of the rest of *Sons and Lovers*. Lawrence sums up this twisted, hurtful marriage (based, again, on his own parents) with amazing detachment, but with a note of sadness perhaps sounding through:

> The pity was, she was too much his opposite. She could not be content with the little he might be; she would have him the much that he ought to be. So, in seeking to make him nobler than he could be, she destroyed him.[21]

I know of no more elegant description in literature of a Pygmalion project.

* * * * *

---

[20] David Keirsey, *Portraits of Temperament*, p. 40.

[21] D.H. Lawrence, *Sons and Lovers*, p. 16.

Walter and Gertrude Morel have, admittedly, a severely distorted relationship. Not often do Artisan-Guardian couples turn on each other with such determined bitterness and violence. But the value of examining such an extreme case is the pattern of truth revealed by the magnification. Because they are so intrinsically opposite, many Artisan-Guardian couples act out Walter and Gertrude's basic cycle of accusation and retaliation, though most on a more benign level, with more patience and restraint, and the relationships right themselves and proceed happily. Still, clearly, Performers are capable of becoming embroiled in quite hurtful Pygmalion projects with their closest loved ones. Performers may share the Sensualists' essentially hedonistic outlook, loving to give pleasure to their public—to "make everyone happy," as Norman would say—but in their personal relationships they are less forgiving than the Sensualists, and seem more disposed to coercive gamesmanship. Though they rarely initiate Pygmalion projects, their need for sexual display is so ever-present, and their desire for social impact is so acute, that when put on too short a leash by an austere partner, or deprived of the spotlight by a disapproving one, Performers will fight back with irritable, spiteful—and usually self-destructive—tactics. In loving a Performer, our wisest course is not to deny them their audience, nor to vie with them for publicity, but to step back when we can and give them center stage, bearing with their exhibitionism and their waywardness—they mean no harm—and taking full pleasure in their irresistible joie de vivre.

Chapter 4
The Instrumentalist

How have you made me into what I am?

—Henrik Ibsen[1]

Keirsey uses the name "Instrumentalist" in the broadest sense to characterize the introverted Operator (whom Myers referred to as the "ISTP"): not simply a player of musical instruments, but an operator of any number of instruments or tools that amplify human capabilities, from the chainsaw to the scalpel, from the earthmover to the race car, from the handgun to the jet fighter. Instrumentalists glory in the speed and command of enhanced physical dexterity, and so become (in Keirsey's phrase) "tool artisans,"[2] or virtuosos with man's most powerful and most dangerous devices. This notion of the "tool artisan" is an unusual view of the artist, and needs perhaps a word of explanation. Keirsey argues in *Please Understand Me* that the fine arts (sculpture, painting, music, dance) are primarily the domain of the graceful Sensualists, but that artistry generally conceived is the

---

[1] Henrik Ibsen, *The Master Builder,* p. 380.

[2] David Keirsey and Marilyn Bates, *Please Understand Me,* p. 201.

mastery of any freely changing physical activity, regardless of the medium. Thus the great gunfighters, pilots, surgeons, builders, and so on are artists in their own right, with that rare ability to fit every move elegantly to their intention, though as Instrumentalists they spend their energy more on speed, power, and conquest than on line and form and graceful composition.

Instrumentalists, of course, can also be fine artists, the arrogant prodigies who regard their musical instruments, their mallets and chisels, or their brushes and palette knives as the tools or even the weapons of fine art. Keirsey cites Michaelangelo and Leonardo da Vinci as examples of the Instrumentalist's fierce—and absolutely typical—insubordination, and indeed my reading suggests that literature, perhaps for the dramatic intensity, views the fine artist at times in this harsher light. John Fowles, for instance, observes the Instrumentalist's tough cynicism in his portrait of Henry Breasley, a legendary (and still quite lecherous) old painter in *The Ebony Tower*. Asked by a young critic why he avoids talking about the sources of his art, Breasley answers with a calculated vulgarity, trying to gall the young intellectual with his somewhat fundamental philosophy of painting:

> "My dear boy. Painted to paint. All my life. Not to give clever young buggers like you a chance to show off. Like shitting, yes? You ask why you do it. How you do it. You die of a blocked arsehole. Don't care a fart in hell where my ideas come from. Never have. Let it happen. That's all. Couldn't even tell you how it starts. What half it means. Don't want to know." He

> nodded back at the Braque. "Old George had a phrase. *Trop de racine.* Yes? Too much root. Origin. Past. Not the flower. The now. Thing on the wall."[3]

Here certainly is the Instrumentalist's tone: cool, playfully antagonistic, charmingly contemptuous, even the clipped sentences expressing Breasley's disdain for the smooth flow of ideas, words, time, for any intellectual abstractions that obscure "the now," the "Thing on the wall." To Breasley, painting is not a matter of Rationalist intellect or Idealist inspiration, nor even a Sensualist's brilliant play with brush and canvas; it is the Instrumentalist's exhilarating struggle to capture the essence of natural form—the thing itself—in all its immediacy.

Gulley Jimson

Fowles's description of the Instrumentalist artist is certainly colorful, but a more sympathetic portrait, with a good deal more insight about love for the Instrumentalist, is Joyce Cary's incorrigible and cantankerous old painter, Gulley Jimson, dictating his memoirs in Cary's wonderful novel, *The Horse's Mouth.*

Much like Henry Breasley, Gulley Jimson is a feisty, cynical old rogue, fed up with intellectual and spiritual pretensions about painting. Gulley says he paints because he likes to, or because he's lazy and hates to work,

---

[3] John Fowles, *The Ebony Tower*, pp. 72-73.

or because he's self-indulgent. And though much of what he says is tactical, meant to offend his more polite listeners and keep them out of his hair, he means what he says about his painting, and he enjoys ridiculing any nobler motivations as only so much schoolboy enthusiasm. Gulley paints not for the mental, but for the sensual satisfaction, claiming, for instance (and describing the Artisan imagination perfectly), that he can feel a painting with his eyes:

> You feel all the rounds, the smooths, the sharp edges, the flats and hollows, the lights and shades, the cools and warms. The colours and textures. There's hundreds of little differences all fitting together.[4]

Gulley also loves to smell and to taste his oils: "Paint. Lovely paint," he croons, "Why I could rub my nose in it or lick it up for breakfast." And he can hear his paintings like musical compositions, what he calls "a sort of coloured music of the mind"; indeed, he worries that one astonishing leg unbalances a group of his figures "like a trumpet in the violins." To Gulley, the painter's imagination is not abstract in any usual sense of the word (as in "imaginary" or "make-believe"), but is what he calls a "Solid imagination," operating in "the real world among the everlasting forms." Painting thus makes visible, not ideas or abstract meanings ("How can you see an idea?" Gulley demands), but "the solid forms of the imagination," the concrete, physical, sensual world of line and color and shape. Gulley is keenly aware of this kaleidoscopic reality, almost constantly observing

---

[4] Joyce Cary, *The Horse's Mouth*, pp. 108-109.

the various shades and contours combining and recombining in the world around him. Gulley often punctuates his narrative with quick, mind's-eye sketches of the London sky and landscape, or of the eternal Thames: "Clouds all in blue and blue-and-soot," he observes, "Blue-black smoke drifting up like smoky candles...and the river pouring quietly along, as bright as ink out of a bottle." Even doodling with a coffee spill, Gulley sees a line that suddenly unifies the figures and colors in his huge mural, *The Fall*:

> One line from nape to croup. A sweet line. I fell for that line....Bring the shoulder forward. Yes, bring his arm right out and have Eve pushing it away....And that nice line will lie right up against the serpent—the serpent will have to come a little behind Adam to avoid two cylinders meeting at the vertical. All right, make the serpent fatter—fatter than Adam. Fat and stiff and erect. And all those red scales against Adam's blue-white flesh.[5]

This extraordinary sensitivity to the slightest variation in a composition, seeing immediately how one shift makes all the parts either conflict or fit perfectly together, is the innate, uncanny gift of the Instrumentalists—and, in their different ways, of all the Artisans.

Although fully at home in his visual and tactile imagination, Gulley has done his share of "arguing and reading and drinking" over the years—when he cannot paint, that is. Indeed, despite claiming that "Talk is not my line....When I've talked a lot, I know I've told a lot of

---

[5] Joyce Cary, *The Horse's Mouth*, p. 24.

lies," various passages in Gulley's memoirs put forth his own anti-intellectual, and thoroughly Artisan view of "good" painting, expressed in his own quirky vocabulary.

The basis of Gulley's philosophy is his belief that the mind can never bring the artist to a good picture, that consciousness must always remain on the outside of the creative process: "Contemplation is not the doings," he insists, "it doesn't get *there*....Contemplation, in fact, is ON THE OUTSIDE. It's not on the spot." And turning contemplation into conversation distances the artist even further from the concrete "spot," his words draining the very life from his picture: "Dangerous to talk too much about your work," he cautions; "it fixes it. It nails it down. And then it bleeds. It begins to die." A good picture, exactly like a good Artisan, must be free to follow its own rules in concrete space, living its own life, sensual and immediate. And the good painter is that gifted individual (and this is precisely the Artisan) who is spontaneous enough, unconscious enough, to escape the ideas and the words, winning through to the silent world of solid forms, "THE INSIDE OF THE OUTSIDE," though perhaps only for moments at a time.

However, once on the inside, past the "surface tricks" and abstract "conjurings" of the mind, the artist gets in touch with the eternal life of the senses, the real "works," as Gulley calls it, struggling to express what he means:

> But what you get on the inside, I said to myself, is the works—it's SOMETHING THAT GOES ON GOING ON. Hold on to that, old boy, I said, for it's the facts of life. It's the ginger in the ginger bread.

> It's the apple in the dumpling....It's the kick in the old horse. It's the creation.[6]

Much like Hemingway or Camus trying to express the concrete world of "things in themselves" in the plainest possible terms, Gulley is almost at a loss for words, describing a good painting as, "It,...a fact,...it's something, almost itself by itself." And thus the good painter, in his moments of inspiration at least, becomes wordless, innocent, sensually attuned, deaf to all but the voice of physical creation, or if mistaken for a spiritual voice, "the pure, innocent song of some damn fool angel that doesn't know even the name of God." Indeed, Gulley's God of painting in the novel is a God of sensual reality, a God made flesh—or horseflesh, rather, since Gulley irreverently refers to Him as the "Old Horse." If the painter can stay in the concrete, in his senses, working in "paint that doesn't mean anything except itself"; if he can block out words and ideas and meanings, learn to "SPEAK ONLY HORSE," as Gully puts it, then his pictures will issue alive and kicking out of the horse's mouth, speaking to us without words about the delight of being alive. As Gulley reminds all us non-Artisans,

> Talk is lies. The only satisfactory form of communication is a good picture. Neither true nor false. But created.[7]

What sets Gulley apart as a specifically Instrumentalist painter, however, is the furious (though often comical) way he engages in this struggle for artistic creativity. To

---

[6] Joyce Cary, *The Horse's Mouth*, p. 113.

[7] Joyce Cary, *The Horse's Mouth*, p. 95.

Gulley, painting is not merely beautiful composition and graceful technique, the Sensualist painter's two distinguishing talents. Gulley admires lovely design, of course, "beauty and so on," as he calls it, and he appreciates the Sensualists' dexterity, their "miracles of brushwork"; but the sweet shapes and the sweet strokes are too polite for his temperament, "just a nice sensation, a little song. Good for the drawing room. Tea cakes." As an Instrumentalist Gulley does not compose or confect his paintings so much as build them or bully them into shape. He wields his "brushes like a carpenter's tools" and he insists on "solid construction" in art as well as life:

> You need to take necessity and make her do what you want; get your feet on her old bones and build your mansions out of her rock....Look at what Mick Angelo did in black and white or a chunk of rock.[8]

Gulley paints pictures not simply to please the eye, but to smack you hard in the face: "a piece of stuff like that, spontaneous," he says of his greatest nude, "brings you bang up against the facts of life." His quick pencil sketches give you "a poke in the belly," and his wall-sized masterpiece, *The Fall*, needs starting over because,

> "It wasn't immediate enough. It didn't hit you hard enough. It wasn't solid enough....No," I said, "what was the Fall after all. The discovery of the solid hard world, good and evil. Hard as rocks and sharp as poisoned thorns."[9]

---

[8] Joyce Cary, *The Horse's Mouth*, p. 59.

[9] Joyce Cary, *The Horse's Mouth*, p. 196.

Gulley wrestles with this huge painting throughout much of *The Horse's Mouth*, and his obsession with the subject matter, mankind's fall from grace, reveals a good deal about the Instrumentalist's cynical attitude toward painting. To the Instrumentalist, painting is not graceful or spiritual play in the garden of Eden, but a bold foray into a disillusioned and dangerous world.

To Gulley, indeed, painting is much like warfare, and he is a master of the devices and maneuvers of the artistic battle. Just securing his supplies is an exercise in Instrumentalist tactical ingenuity. A natural scrounger, Gulley deftly shoplifts his brushes and oilpots, and when unable to "borrow" his large canvases, he resorts to cunning verbal subterfuge. He first asks the shopkeeper for something else: "It causes the enemy to concentrate on the wrong flank," he schemes, "and upsets his communications." However, if the shopkeeper is on guard against such feints, Gulley shifts to a confusing give-and-take over price: "So that the enemy doesn't know whether you're advancing backwards or he's retreating forwards, or you're retreating forwards while he's advancing to fresh positions in the rear." This is no gentlemanly exchange of fire nor any long-range strategic planning (types of warfare instinctive to other temperaments), but an Instrumentalist's spur-of-the-moment, seat-of-the-pants outfoxing of an opponent—any trick so long as the enemy "hasn't time to look up the rules of war; or if he does remember them he can't quite see how they apply to the situation."

Not only negotiating the equipment, but painting the picture itself is a pitched battle for Gulley. When starting a new wall painting, with the surface freshly whitened and his vision intact, before the paint goes on and the creative struggle begins, Gulley feels all the glory and optimism of a military commander:

> No admiral on the bridge of a new battleship designed by the old navy, could feel more pleased with himself than Gulley, on two planks, forty feet above dirt level, with his palette table beside him, his brush in his hand, and the draught blowing up his trousers; cleared for action.[10]

Keeping a painting solidly imaginative, however, may call for more violent action, and Gulley is known to bully his models in his frustration with a picture. Working with Sara Monday, for example, he "didn't know whether to draw her or bite her," and he only succeeds in capturing the essential female in her by beating down the individual woman, prodding her with his back brush and tapping her "on the neb" to tame her for his use. Gulley also bullies the shapes and colors in his pictures, trying to keep them from fading and dying on him, or from swelling into pretentious illusions: he brushes in a "clash in the reds" to bring one painting to life, he knocks formulaic Cubist shapes "down with hammers" in another, and in one particularly difficult drawing he imagines his shapes lining up against him like "a row of fists." Fortunately (and unlike the gentler Sensualists), Instrumentalists seem to enjoy these hostilities; as Gulley reminisces of his years with Sara: "Painting her and fighting her...what a life."

---

[10] Joyce Cary, *The Horse's Mouth*, p. 312.

In short, Gulley's way with a painting, is concrete, tactical, and belligerent, and one of Joyce Cary's great insights into the Instrumentalist character is that Gulley's way with women in much the same. At bottom, women simply don't exist for Gulley if they don't contribute concretely to his painting. Early in his career, he confesses, he was so desperate to get his figures right that "I hardly noticed when...my wife went off, or even when my mother died." Indeed, Gulley sees women more as anatomical models for his pictures ("spiritual fodder" he calls them) than as persons or intimate relations. Gulley thus covets his homely little friend Coker for her powerful "marble" elbow: "The sweetest elbow I ever saw, and that's a difficult joint...I could have kissed Coker for that elbow." On his honeymoon with Sara Monday, he was more interested in getting her down on canvas than getting her into bed: "Just keep like that a minute, Sara, while I catch the slant of the left shoulder." And Gulley was first attracted to Sara's best friend Rozzie (with whom he has an affair) for her mammoth body: "You studied her from different aspects," he remembers fondly, "like a public building." Gulley dismisses abstract, spiritual women, on the other hand, as mere sentimental decorations, obscuring men's vision with their romantic expectations. Thus he turns a romantic scene of a young woman walking with her boyfriend into a cynical mental sketch of deception and entrapment:

> Girl going past clinging to a young man's arm. Putting up her face like a duck to the moon. Drinking joy. Green in her eyes. Spinal curvature. No chin, mouth like a frog. Young man like a pug. Gazing down at his sweetie with the face of a saint reading the works of God. Hold

> on, maiden, you've got him. He's your boy....Nail him, girlie. Nail him to the contract.[11]

Gulley delights in women—to be sure, he has trouble leaving them alone—but they must be solid women, strong, fleshy female shapes, useful in his work, figures of the fallen Eve, not clinging London girlies with their sweet illusions thinly camouflaging their agenda for control.

Gulley, in fact, operates on exactly the opposite assumption: that the only proper role for a man, as an artist or as a lover, is free and strong and in charge of the woman—a Pygmalion sculpting his Galatea. Indeed, Gulley describes the whole enterprise of painting as capturing "the maiden" of physical form, not so much by seducing her (the Sensualist's forté), as by dominating her, chaining her, getting your "maiden under padlock," as he puts it. Cézanne had as much success as anyone, Gulley believes, though even Cézanne's maiden was hard to pin down and "fled away so fast that he hardly caught her once a year." The female is coy, in life as well as in art, and the Instrumentalist male needs all his tactical intelligence, and all his physical strength, to defeat her and shape her to his vision. Gulley knows, for instance, that if Coker ever stops falling for his charming lies (and helping him with money, a bed, and so on), he will have to persuade her with force, and a sculptor's tools: "next time I have to deal with Coker on the level," he figures,

---

[11] Joyce Cary, *The Horse's Mouth*, pp. 50-51.

"I'll take a hammer with me." Gulley also remembers his marriage with Sara Monday as a time of glorious masculine conquest:

> It was a glory to have that woman, and to beat her. Alexander never felt bigger than me when I thumped that majestic meat upon the nose.[12]

And when he sees Sara again years later, showing her age but still putting on her airs, he is almost overcome by the desire to smack her, just to remind her who's the boss:

> I had the old feeling all over again. I wanted to give her a tap....Not a hard one. She wasn't my wife any more. But just a tap, platonic....Just to bring to her attention the existence of the forgotten man.[13]

And so, as he watches Sara pose and primp, and listens to her familiar sweet-talk, Gulley (ever the tactician) moves in for a better angle of attack: "I pulled my chair up nearer. Took up a strategic position on the left flank."

Indeed, Sara has been Gulley's chief adversary in love—and Pygmalion projects—over the years. Sara is a Performer Artisan who has always lived for her pleasures ("I do like people that know how to enjoy themselves, man or boy"), but who has carefully safeguarded her reputation with a public show of Guardian modesty and virtue: "Sara could commit adultery at one end," Gulley tells us,

---

[12] Joyce Cary, *The Horse's Mouth*, p. 291.

[13] Joyce Cary, *The Horse's Mouth*, pp. 31, 33.

"and weep for her sins at the other, and enjoy both operations at once." Sara married Gulley for his liveliness and "gaiety," but quickly learned on their honeymoon that her husband's real love was the "maiden" of his painting, and that he was more interested in her as a voluptuous shape than as a bride: "I could never make out whether it was me or my flesh that you wanted—that was the beginning of all our trouble." On his side, Gulley married Sara for her maternal Guardian facade: "I fell in love with Mrs. Monday, the mother and the wife," he admits; "I wanted to rest upon the domestic bosom." And he remembers their honeymoon quite differently: "Who made the trouble?" he demands; "It was nag, nag, nag." Gulley insists that, after the wedding, Sara tried to assert control over him, hoping in her vanity to vanquish the rival maiden of his art, and to make Gulley faithful to her alone. She tried "to button up," as Gulley sees it, his bold, artistic impulse with "all those tactful arrangements and nice comfortable little formulas," becoming a "tyrant who tried to put me in a bottle and cork me up into a woman's cup of tea." Gulley would not be "a meal for any old wife," however, and his instinctive Instrumentalist response was to retaliate[14]—

---

[14] Gulley's violent temper yearns for retaliation many times in *The Horse's Mouth*. For example, after being beaten by a man he has just tried to swindle, Gulley collects himself, tries to remember his blood pressure, and plots his revenge:

> Forgive and forget. Till you have him set. Remember that he had a certain amount of excuse for his actions. Give him his due, but not till you are ready with a crowbar. Don't get spiteful. Keep cool....Approach the matter in a judicious spirit, meet him with a friendly smile, and a couple of knuckledusters. Don't let him get on your nerves...but get on his face and push it through his backbone (pp. 262-263).

to fight for his freedom—both by slapping Sara around ("It was the only way to teach you to keep out of my business"), and by sneaking off to Rozzie (a more dependable Guardian) for more sincere motherly comforting. Gulley and Sara wage their war for control through all the years of their marriage, Sara flirting and goading to get her way, all the time playing the innocent, and Gulley taking his abusive revenge, actually enjoying what he regards as a "challenge to battle and death."

In the end, Sara seems to understand Gulley's impulsiveness and waywardness, and (after their long separation, at least) she holds no grudge. When they meet again in *The Horse's Mouth*, they share a few pints and talk over old times and old battles:

> "You broke my nose and I came back to you. And the times you pinched me and stuck pins in my poor behind, long ones, I wonder how I stood it. You were a cruel husband, Gulley." "You were a bad woman, Sall." "God knows I had my faults, but...wasn't it all for your pleasure?"[15]

Gulley's answer to this question, framed in many ways throughout his narrative, reveals the colder heart of love for the Instrumentalist. To Sara, after all is said and done, physical pleasure is enough in love and in life; but to Gulley, the essence of his life is his "lovely" work, the adventure of his painting, the tools, the tactics, the struggles and the thrills of making good pictures. He

[15] Joyce Cary, *The Horse's Mouth*, p. 218.

announces on the first page of the novel, establishing his more impatient Instrumentalist tone, "I hadn't time to waste on pleasure. A man of my age has to get on with the job." And at the end, as he suffers a stroke, barely clinging to his scaffolding, he lapses into a long hallucination, dreaming that Sara is still interfering with his work, and that he is still fighting her to the death:

> Now, Sall, you go away. You get off. I've got a job on—the biggest job of my life. And I've got to finish it....I'm getting in the forms and the tones, and I've no time to waste.[16]

In a word, Instrumentalists love action more than pleasure, and (more than any other type) they are compelled do their "thing," do it continuously and relentlessly—"keep on keeping on" in Gulley's famous phrase—not out of devotion to the job, nor simply for the sensual pleasure of it, but out of a passionate pride in their virtuosity with instruments and an overwhelming urge for power and victory.

Hedda Gabler

As Gulley Jimson's unabashed male chauvinism abundantly illustrates, the Instrumentalist's world has historically been the masculine domain in our culture. The Instrumentalists' tool skills, their love of danger and violence, triumph and power, have long been considered

---

[16] Joyce Cary, *The Horse's Mouth*, p. 336.

innately masculine characteristics, and only recently have women found their way into the traditional Instrumentalist professions (soldiering, piloting, constructing, policing, etc.), or into the favorite Instrumentalist recreations (racing, hunting, piloting, etc.). For centuries, peaking in the nineteenth century Victorian era, female Instrumentalists were kept in the home, locked in the kitchen or the nursery, so to speak, able to experience the bold, exciting world of power and conquest only through the exploits of their husbands or their male children. And all too often female Instrumentalists had to satisfy their hunger for action by becoming Pygmalions, manipulating their husbands and sons into companion Artisans, not only for the vicarious excitement this might bring them, but for their own, small thrill of conquering a man. Such longstanding, systematic repression took a terrible toll on female Instrumentalists, on their personal lives and on their families, and only at the end of the nineteenth century did literature begin to count the cost. Henrik Ibsen's brooding play *Hedda Gabler* is such an account, presenting one of the most disturbing portraits in western literature of a powerful woman struggling desperately against her culture to express her Instrumentalist temperament.

From Hedda's initial appearance in the play, Ibsen carefully differentiates her from the polite, sentimental Victorian world around her. Although she is celebrated as "The beautiful Hedda Gabler," her beauty is more trenchant and arrogant, perhaps even masculine, than the softly feminine, curly blond Victorian ideal. Ibsen's stage directions on Hedda's entrance immediately establish her character as strangely icy and formidable:

> *...her complexion is pallid and opaque. Her steel gray eyes express a cool, unruffled calm. Her hair is an attractive medium brown, but not particularly abundant...*[17]

Also, Ibsen often directs that Hedda's lines be spoken with a "*scornful smile,*" with "*cold constraint,*" or with a "*disdainful gesture,*" and the main object of her contempt is clearly the well-meaning but conventional world of Victorian propriety. Indeed, as the play opens, Hedda has just returned from her honeymoon with George Tesman, a timid, dutiful history scholar (an "SJ" Guardian), and though she tries to play the charming and gracious bride, she cannot help treating her new home and her new family with a barely suppressed ridicule. She keeps George coldly at arm's length, allowing him a few, awkward familiarities, but denying him any security or pride in her love: "Love? You *are* absurd," she says of her wifely feelings; "don't use that syrupy word!" And after George's Auntie Julie (another ministering Guardian) gives Hedda a rather ceremonial welcome home, Hedda cruelly insults her, calling Julie's fashionable new hat (which she bought just to please Hedda) some ugly old thing the maid had left lying about. Julie tries to forgive Hedda the faux pas with an almost sacramental embrace, bending Hedda's head down gently and kissing her hair, but Hedda cannot stand the confinement, nor the sentimentality, and pushes her

---

[17] Henrik Ibsen, *Hedda Gabler*, p. 228.

away: "Oh—!" she shudders, "Let me go." Asked later how she could bring herself to hurt that "fine old lady," Hedda haltingly explains the Instrumentalist's overpowering impulse to attack: "Well, it's—these things come over me, just like that, suddenly. And I can't hold back."

Hedda's impulsiveness can be more violent, as well, and she expresses her fury with one of the Instrumentalist's favorite devices, the gun. Hedda's most cherished gift from her dead father, the handsome, wicked old General Gabler, is a brace of duelling pistols, which she handles with defiant pride, as if their explosive power lifts her above the ordinary, demure Victorian woman. Thus, when George's appointment to the university seems in jeopardy, and she may have to give up her riding horse, Hedda turns to her pistols for comfort and excitement:

> HEDDA (*crossing the room*). Well, at least I have one thing left to amuse myself with.
> TESMAN (*beaming*). Ah, thank heaven for that! What is it, Hedda? Uh?
> HEDDA (*in the center of the doorway, looking at him with veiled scorn*). My pistols, George.
> TESMAN (*in fright*). Your pistols!
> HEDDA (*her eyes cold*). General Gabler's pistols.[18]

Hedda resents the impotence of Victorian women, particularly their sexual intimidation, and her pistols, as masculine objects imbued with her father's sense of command, enable her to play out some measure of

---

[18] Henrik Ibsen, *Hedda Gabler*, p. 247.

revenge. For example, when Judge Brack (a Promoter Artisan, and one of her most lecherous admirers) approaches through the garden, she quickly asserts her control over the relationship by pretending to use him for target practice:

> HEDDA (*raises the pistol and aims*). And now, Judge, I'm going to shoot you!
> BRACK (*shouting from below*). No-no-no! Don't point that thing at me!
> HEDDA. That's what comes from sneaking in the back way. (*she fires.*)
> BRACK (*nearer*). Are you out of your mind—!
> HEDDA. Oh, dear—I didn't hit you, did I?[19]

When the Judge manages to reach the house safely, he (the Victorian Man) tries to put Hedda in her place, scolding her like a little girl for her carelessness: "Good God!" he chides her, "Are you still playing such games?" In some sense Hedda *is*, like all the Artisans, a little child playing with her toys; but more deeply, she is a frustrated female Instrumentalist injecting some thrill of danger and competition into her hopelessly boring Victorian existence: "Well," she demands of Brack, returning fire in what is now a verbal skirmish, "what in heaven's name do you want me to do with myself?"

As an Instrumentalist, Hedda longs for action and adventure, for speed and power, not the civilities—the "absurdities," as she calls them—she has settled for as a Victorian woman. Several times in the play Ibsen con-

---

[19] Henrik Ibsen, *Hedda Gabler*, p. 248.

fuses Hedda with a notorious prostitute, one "Mademoiselle Diana...a mighty huntress—of men." In mythology, Diana was the goddess of the hunt and wild things, and in some ways the feminine side of Dionysus ("Dian"/ "Dion"), the totem deity of all the Artisans. Much like Dionysus' frenzied female worshippers (the Bacchae), Diana would flash through the forest, ruthlessly wielding her weapons, more free and powerful than any man, exactly Hedda's ideal as she grew up. In school she teased a young girl (her rival, a prim little blond) by pulling the girl's hair, and threatening to "burn it off." As a young girl she could be seen "out with her father...galloping past in that long black riding outfit, with a feather in her hat." And before her marriage to Tesman, Hedda quietly sought out "beautiful and fascinating—and daring" friendships with romantic men, trying to catch "some glimpse a world that...she's forbidden to know anything about." Hedda was repressed enough to be deathly afraid of public scandal, and yet her Dionysian nature longed for recognition and fraternity. She first joined secretly with Eilert Løvborg, a young "NF" Idealist, in a passionate "companionship in a thirst for life," meeting with him and asking him "such questions....So boldly" about his drinking and his sexual freedom. And after Løvborg lost control of himself, fleeing to the country in disgrace, Hedda quietly entered Judge Brack's risqué bachelor circle, hoping to escape the boredom of feminine domesticity.

As a grown woman in need of a respectable marriage, however, Hedda denied her "hunger for life," let Løvborg and Brack go their own ways, and settled on George

Tesman, whose great talent, she discovers, is collecting and ordering obscure historical documents, and who spent most of their honeymoon rummaging around in European libraries. Soon after the play opens, then, Hedda finds herself no more a wild, free Diana, but a dutiful Victorian wife, bound "everlastingly together with—with one and the same person," trapped in a house that smells of decay, "like a corsage," as she puts it, "the day after the dance." Hedda realizes full well "how horribly I'm going to bore myself" in her marriage, and she paces her Victorian drawing room like a caged wild animal panting for her freedom:

> ...HEDDA *moves about the room, raising her arms and clenching her fists as if in a frenzy. Then she flings back the curtains from the glass door and stands there, looking out.*[20]

Staring at the garden, as if regarding a paradise lost, Hedda no longer sees the riotous colors of spring, but the pall of her September existence: "I'm just looking at the leaves—" she explains, revealing her own disappointment, "they're so yellow—and so withered."

Hedda's decision to marry Tesman, to commit herself to this withering Victorian world, seems incomprehensible to nearly everyone in the play—including Tesman—but makes perfect sense as an Instrumentalist's Pygmalion project. Hedda was drawn to Tesman in the first place because he was in so many ways her opposite. Tesman (a thoroughgoing Guardian) is nothing in life if not careful and responsible, fussing after the honeymoon about his

---

[20] Henrik Ibsen, *Hedda Gabler*, p. 231.

"suitcase stuffed full of notes," rejoicing when he finds the bedroom slippers that he missed so much on the trip, and worrying about his new professorship—about "how people are going to make a living." And Tesman loves to take care of Hedda, pleasing her and serving her: he insisted that Hedda have her expensive honeymoon tour, he sacrificed to buy Hedda the expensive town house she said she wanted, and he happily sees to her every physical comfort, gushing "I think it's such fun to wait on you." For her part, Hedda likes to have her way and to be fawned over, as she explains to an amused Judge Brack: "when [Tesman] kept pressing and pleading to be allowed to take care of me—I didn't see why I ought to resist." Hedda also likes the safety and stability Tesman offers her. Though he isn't "at all amusing to travel with," he is "thoroughly acceptable" as a husband, "and dependable, beyond a doubt." After her scandalous youth, Hedda admits reluctantly that she was ready to settle down ("I really had danced myself out"), and though Tesman sometimes embarrasses her with his stiff, over-serious manner, she admires him as a "man of such learning," and she insists, almost as if convincing herself of his virtue, that "he works incredibly hard on his research." As I have explained, Artisan-Guardian marriages often balance out beautifully, and if Hedda could have contented herself with Tesman's conscientious devotion, resting in his safe harbor, she might have found the patience to survive.

Unfortunately, Hedda also married Tesman for what she could make of him, and her attempt at a Pygmalion project only adds to her bitter frustration. Her plan for the marriage was to have an extravagant, socially brilliant time, in other words, to turn her cautious Guardian husband into an impulsive Artisan like herself, a free spender who would pay for all her whims. Hedda wanted a butler and a riding horse and a new, expensive piano; she wanted to play "hostess" at grand parties and to have impressive social impact: "It was part of our bargain," Hedda reminds Tesman, "that we'd live in society—that we'd keep a great house." She schemed as well that she could take the bookish young history professor and encourage him to enter the aggressive world of politics, even if against his Guardian temperament:

> HEDDA. I was thinking—if I could get Tesman to go into politics.
> BRACK (*laughing*). Tesman! No, I can promise you—politics is absolutely out of his line.
> HEDDA. No, I can believe you. But even so, I wonder if I could get him into it?
> BRACK. Well, what satisfaction would you have in that, if he can't succeed? Why push him in that direction?
> HEDDA. Because, I told you, I'm bored! (*After a pause.*) Then you think it's really out of the question that he could ever be a cabinet minister?[21]

Hedda married Tesman, in short, for the challenge of changing him, for the excitement of a Pygmalion project, but soon after the marriage, as she comes to know more intimately the essential domesticity of the Guardian, she realizes how terribly she has miscalculated. Tesman is endlessly cooperative, but far too guilt-ridden and shy

---

[21] Henrik Ibsen, *Hedda Gabler*, pp. 255-256.

ever to succeed in the ambitious role she had planned for him. And as she tastes the bitter consequences of her rashness, understanding just how trapped she is, her Instrumentalist nature seethes with suppressed rage:

> HEDDA (*rising impatiently*). Yes, there it is! It's this tight little world I've stumbled into—(*crossing the room.*) That's what make life so miserable! So utterly ludicrous! Because that's what it *is*.[22]

Had Ibsen left Hedda simply to cope with a disappointing marriage, the play would have unravelled quickly into an ordinary domestic melodrama, a Victorian soap opera of sorts. Indeed, in classic soap style, Hedda quietly nurses her agenda for Tesman ("There's every chance that, in time, he could still make a name for himself"); and just to keep life interesting she coyly agrees to resume her relationship with Judge Brack, in what he calls a "kind of—let's say, triangular arrangement." But Ibsen raises the stakes, and the tenor of the drama, by offering Hedda another Pygmalion project, one which promises her some release from her tight little world, but which ends in tragedy. The plot thickens when Eilert Løvborg returns from the country cured of his dissipation, and apparently ready to challenge Tesman for his appointment to the university. At first, Hedda is amused by the prospect of a competition: "Just think, Tesman—it will be like a kind of championship match." But when she understands just how thoroughly Løvborg has changed—a change she regards as nothing less than a

---

[22] Henrik Ibsen, *Hedda Gabler*, p. 256.

defection from their secret past—she takes up her hammer and chisel with a vengeance.

Years before, Hedda had thrilled to Løvborg's desperate confessions, "About the way I'd go out, the drinking, the madness that went on day and night, for days at a time," and she had gloried in her command over such a Dionysus, as she thought of him: "Ah, what power was it in you, Hedda, that made me tell you such things?" But now Løvborg appears rededicated and idealistic, "Firm as a rock. True to principle," and eager "to build up my position again—and try to make a fresh start." (Løvborg is a superb example of an Idealist wrestling with his dark, satanic side—what the Jungians call his "shadow"—a struggle I will detail in Volume Four.) Even worse, Løvborg has fallen under the beneficent spell of Thea Elvsted, Hedda's blond little rival from school. Thea is another Guardian in the play, and she has rehabilitated Løvborg's insane excesses, inspiring his brilliant new book (a theoretical treatise on the future of society), which Thea thinks of as the "little child" of their love. Hedda cannot believe that Løvborg, once her daring companion, is now a productive, even prophetic member of the Victorian world; indeed, her own sense of freedom is diminished—her world tightened a bit more—by Løvborg's betrayal of his Dionysian youth. And so, contemptuous of his cowardly change of heart (but also excited by a challenge to her power), Hedda sets out systematically and cynically to restore Løvborg's thirst for life.

Hedda's first move is to destroy "little Thea's" influence by hinting to Løvborg just how little faith Thea had in his rehabilitation. Hedda has the Instrumentalist's uncanny ability to sense and to exploit others' vulnerability,[23] and in an unbelievably cruel display of interpersonal manipulation, she "innocently" ruins both Løvborg's trust in Thea and his hard-won sobriety:

> HEDDA (*turning to* MRS. ELVSTED *and patting her*). Well, now, didn't I tell you that [Løvborg was in no danger] when you came here so distraught this morning—
> LØVBORG (*surprised*). Distraught?
> MRS. ELVSTED (*terrified*). Hedda–! But Hedda–!
> HEDDA. Can't you see for yourself? There's no need at all for your going around so deathly afraid that—(*Changing her tone.*) Now we can all enjoy ourselves.
> LØVBORG (*shaken*). What is all this , Mrs. Tesman?
> MRS. ELVSTED. Oh, God, oh God, Hedda! What are you saying! What are you doing...
> LØVBORG (*looks intently at her a moment, his face drawn*). So that's how completely you trusted me...(*takes one of the glasses of punch, raises it, and says in a low, hoarse voice*). Your health, Thea! (*He empties the glass, puts it down, and takes the other.*)
> MRS. ELVSTED (*imploringly*). Oh, Hedda, Hedda—how could you want such a thing!
> HEDDA. Want it? I? Are you crazy?
> LØVBORG. And your health too, Mrs. Tesman. Thanks for the truth. Long live truth! (*Drains the glass and starts to refill it.*)[24]

---

[23] David S. Janowsky, et al., "Playing the Manic Game," *Archives of General Psychiatry*, Vol. 22, March, 1970, pp. 254-256. Note the authors' general finding: "In interpersonal encounters, the manic possesses a highly refined talent for sensing an individual's vulnerability or a group's area of conflict, and exploiting this in a manipulative fashion..." (p. 254).

[24] Henrik Ibsen, *Hedda Gabler*, pp. 268-269.

This is a virtuoso performance for Hedda. In one deft, spontaneous stroke she accomplishes her two objectives, winning her way with two characters, while almost entirely shifting the blame from her own shoulders. After her embarrassing failure with Tesman, Hedda admits that this time, "For once in my life, I want to have power over a human being," and indeed she has asserted her power over two. Thea has been effectively checkmated, and to signify her capture Hedda encloses her bodily ("*passionately throws her arms around her*") and exults, "I think I'll burn your hair off, after all!" At the same time, Løvborg appears once again a "free man," a born-again Dionysian, and Hedda sends him off to Judge Brack's drunken stag party, picturing him "with vine leaves in his hair—fiery and bold."

Victorian propriety thwarts Hedda at every turn, however, and, as the Guardian world tightens its grip, her own maneuvers grow more drastic. Brack's stag party, which Hedda envisioned as a magnificent Dionysian revel celebrating Løvborg's release, turns into a drunken free-for-all at Mademoiselle Diana's parlors, an embarrassing scandal broken up by the police and calling for a public investigation. Løvborg's reputation is ruined once again, and he returns to Hedda stripped of his crown of vine leaves, and confessing that Thea still controls him: "It's the courage and daring for life—that's what she's broken in me." Hedda feels her power slipping away, and her tactics this time border on the malevolent. Acting with a twisted Artisan impulse, she encourages Løvborg to commit suicide, and she pleads with him to "arrange that—that it's done beautifully...for this once...promise me," even providing him with one of her pistols to seal the bargain. In other words, if Hedda can no longer live through Løvborg's dissolution, she will defy the Victorian world through his destruction: "HEDDA (*in a clear bold voice*). 'At last, something truly done... there's beauty in all this.'" And finally, hoping to sever Thea's ties to Løvborg once and for all, Hedda literally dismembers their progenic manuscript, feeding page after page to the fire, in a terrifying scene of hypnotic, almost satanic incantation:

> HEDDA (*throwing some of the sheets into the fire and whispering to herself*). Now I'm burning your child, Thea! You with your curly hair! (*throwing another sheaf in the stove.*) Your child and Eilert Løvborg's. (*throwing in the rest.*) Now I'm burning—I'm burning the child.[25]

Keirsey calls the Instrumentalists, in their darkest impulses, "sadistic manics" who take revenge on their enemies, and furnish themselves with excitement at the same time, by "trampling on the values of others...or injuring something valued."[26] Certainly Hedda, as she struggles to maintain her power over Løvborg and Thea, fits this description all too well.

After so much frustration, Hedda's final disappointment seems little more than the last, inevitable blow of some punitive Victorian nemesis. Løvborg is indeed shot, and Hedda at first glows with the knowledge: "It's liberating

---

[25] Henrik Ibsen, *Hedda Gabler*, p. 288.

[26] David Keirsey, *Portraits of Temperament*, p. 28.

to know," she announces, "that there can still actually be a free and courageous action in this world. Something that shimmers with spontaneous beauty." And she swells with pride that Løvborg, "had the strength and the will to break away from the banquet of life—so young." But when Judge Brack reports the sordid facts of the incident, that the pistol discharged during a tussle in Mademoiselle Diana's boudoir, and that a police investigation has already been mounted, Hedda collapses with revulsion: "What is it," she demands of her fate, "this—this curse—that everything I touch turns ridiculous and vile?"

Hedda has more to fear from the Victorian world than scandal, however. Tesman cautions her that burning Løvborg's manuscript was "illegal disposition of lost property"; and Brack implies that by giving Løvborg the pistol Hedda became an accomplice in his death, a bit of information he will happily withhold from the police—in exchange for personal favors, that is. What's worse, Hedda has finally acknowledged to Tesman that she is pregnant, a development she has denied throughout the play, detesting the commitment involved ("I won't have responsibilities!" she cries), and resenting even more the obvious evidence that Tesman—any man, for that matter—has mastered her. And so, at the end, as she faces the galling truth of the "tight little world" closing in, Hedda recoils with a prophetic despair: "(*clenching her fists*) Oh, I'll die—I'll die of all this!"

Thus trapped on every side by the masculine Victorian world, Hedda confronts perhaps the ultimate interpersonal horror for the female Instrumentalist: "I'm in your power," she tells Judge Brack, "Tied to your will and desire. Not free. Not free, then! (*Rises impetuously.*) No—I can't bear the thought of it. Never!" And so, to wrest her freedom from the Victorian men and the Victorian laws, as well as from the Aunties and the babies and the curly blonds, Hedda finds herself drawn irresistibly to a final act of insubordination. With all other avenues of expression denied her, she moves majestically behind a curtain to her piano, plays "a wild dance melody" as if to announce her defiance, and then takes her remaining pistol and shoots herself in the temple—"beautifully," as she must have believed.

Hedda's suicide, let me emphasize, is a highly unusual end for an Instrumentalist. It is true that their affinity for weapons and their love of powerful machines make Instrumentalists perhaps the most reckless of all the Artisans, and all too often they put themselves in dangerous situations, and meet a violent death in a shooting mishap, racing accident, motorcycle crash, or the like. However, suicide is not a careless act, and though Instrumentalists are known to threaten suicide as a tactical ploy in their relationships, studies in behavioral science have shown that they rarely follow through.[27] But in Hedda's case (and this is precisely Ibsen's indictment of the Victorian world), the repression of her Dionysian instincts is so complete—she is so impossibly cornered—that she feels she must seize her freedom in a last, perversely artistic assertion of victory.

* * * * *

---

[27] See Hervey Cleckley's discussion of suicidal tendencies in the psychopathologic personality in *The Mask of Sanity*, p. 393.

Even more than most literary characters, certainly, Hedda Gabler is an extreme case study, forced to the limits of her temperament to dramatize what Ibsen saw as the tragedy of Artisan women in repressive Victorian culture. In real life (and in contemporary culture), female Instrumentalists rarely remain in such a twisted set of relationships long enough to be driven to deliberate self-destruction. Still, male or female, Instrumentalists are more contentious than their Sensualist or Performer cousins, and their Pygmalion projects are clearly more assertive. Keirsey sees the Instrumentalists as "proactive in defining role relationships,"[28] which means they are quite comfortable taking charge of a relationship, and quite forceful in shaping their loved ones the way they want them. In a word, Instrumentalists are not so much hedonistic as utilitarian—their first impulse is not for sensual pleasure but for tactical success—and partners who try to tame their aggressiveness or belittle their victories, who somehow frustrate the Instrumentalist's need to be top gun, can be met with cunning retaliation. In loving an Instrumentalist, our wisest course is not to badger them for tenderness and thoughtfulness, nor to begrudge them their tools and their adventures, but to provide them with a stable, tolerant home, understanding their single-minded passion for perfecting their skills, and appreciating—no matter how one-sided this may seem—their extraordinary virtuosity.

---

[28] David Keirsey, *Portraits of Temperament*, p. 18.

Chapter 5 The Promoter

> *And so I tell this tale to every man,*
> *"It's all for sale and let him win who can."*
>
> —Geoffrey Chaucer[1]

If the Instrumentalists are experts at operating the tools and machines that extend their own faculties, the more gregarious Promoters (whom Myers called the "ESTP"s) are, as Keirsey describes them, "master manipulators of the external environment,"[2] particularly skillful at maneuvering the men and women around them—their friends and enemies in personal relationships, their associates and opponents in business dealings. Witty, charming, and cocksure, coolly in charge of the moment, one eye always sizing up their audience, always smoothing their approach, Promoters have an uncanny ability to inspire confidence in their partners, be they economic or romantic. Indeed, Promoters are by nature confidence men (and women), the irresistible entrepreneur, negotiator, or salesman on one side of the law, the clever

---

[1] Geoffrey Chaucer, "The Wife of Bath's Prologue" in *The Canterbury Tales,* Nevill Coghill trans., p. 226.

[2] David Keirsey and Marilyn Bates, *Please Understand Me,* p. 196.

swindler, bunko "artist," or racketeer on the other. And in love, Promoters are perhaps the most artful Pygmalions of all the Artisans, finding in the manipulative process itself an almost aesthetic pleasure. They are thus master "chiselers" in both senses of the word, with the con-man's larcenous instincts as well as the Artisan's innate ability to shape the concrete world. Sculpting a loved one, like forming a business merger or pulling off a sting, is an exciting but also a highly aggressive venture, and Promoters embark on such an enterprise not only with the thrill of battle, but with an unrelenting determination to succeed.

Jay Gatsby

F. Scott Fitzgerald captures these two sides of the Promoter, the duplicity as well as the determination, the charm as well as the ambition, in Jay Gatsby, the legendary hero of his celebrated novel of the Jazz Age, *The Great Gatsby*. Keirsey observes in *Please Understand Me* that Promoters "are usually somewhat of a mystery to their mates and to others,"[3] and indeed, to most of New York society, Gatsby is a figure of fabulous—and scandalous—speculation. Gatsby lives alone in a colossal mansion on Long Island Sound and gives extravagant, sumptuous, seemingly interminable parties, overwhelming his guests with tables of exotic food, trays of cocktails, tipsy showgirls, and blaring orchestras. His guests and hangers-on, however, seem even more amused gossiping drunkenly about his character. Some believe

[3] David Keirsey and Marilyn Bates, *Please Understand Me*, p. 198.

he's a bootlegger, others insist "he's a nephew or a cousin of Kaiser Wilhelm's"; one girl whispers, enthralled, "Somebody told me they thought he killed a man," but another is more cautious, preferring the rumor that "he was a German spy during the war." The Promoter's identity is innately fluid, opportunistic, chameleon-like, and certainly Gatsby has this intriguing knack of living in the eye of the beholder, letting himself be whatever his guests want him to be.

But Gatsby is also adept at the other side of this interpersonal confidence game: he makes you believe in some ideal version of yourself in order to gain your trust, promoting your self-esteem for his own advantage.[4] Thus, when Nick Carraway, the idealistic narrator of the novel, first meets Gatsby at one of his gala parties, Gatsby quickly charms him with his beguiling smile:

> He smiled understandingly—much more than understandingly. It was one of those rare smiles with a quality of eternal reassurance in it....It faced—or seemed to face—the whole external world for an instant, and then concentrated on *you* with an irresistible prejudice in your favor. It understood you just as far as you wanted to be understood, believed in you as you would like to believe in yourself, and assured you that it had precisely the impression of you that, at your best, you hoped to convey.[5]

---

[4] David S. Janowsky, et al., "Playing the Manic Game," *Archives of General Psychiatry*, Vol. 22, March, 1970, pp. 253-254. The authors observe, "The manic individual, with extraverted drive...seems friendly, bright, cheerful, resourceful, and entertaining. He is talented in sensing what form of attention or flattery appeals to others" (p. 253).

[5] F. Scott Fitzgerald, *The Great Gatsby*, p. 48.

Though Nick is an Idealist (and will come in the course of the novel to believe in Gatsby and to romanticize him considerably), he is not quite taken in at this first meeting. He shakes off Gatsby's smile, and regains enough presence of mind to describe his host as "an elegant young roughneck, a year or two over thirty, whose elaborate formality of speech just missed being absurd." Still, when Gatsby suddenly vanishes, called by his butler to the wire, Nick is left, like all the other guests, to wonder about the "real" Gatsby: "Who is he?" Nick demands, "Where is he from, I mean? And what does he do?"

Gatsby's identity is such a mystery—he seems so unreal, so fantastically invented—because his life is so much more a matter of gesture and flourish than of substance. Nick describes Gatsby's Promoter temperament with wonderful clarity: "If personality is an unbroken series of successful gestures, then there was something gorgeous about him." And, to be sure, Gatsby goes about life advertising his urbanity with a "gorgeous" pretentiousness. He tells people he's an "Oxford man," and he speaks, as Nick observed, with an affected sophistication: "Good morning, old sport." He name-drops with just the right reluctance, cops and crooks alike: he tells Nick the police commissioner sends him "a Christmas card every year," and that he lunches with "the man who fixed the World's Series back in 1919." He casually flaunts his hydroplane and his elegant new convertible (cream colored, with green leather upholstery): "It's pretty, isn't it, old sport!" He signs his party invitations with "a majestic hand," and surprises his guests with luxurious gifts: when one woman tears her skirt at a party, Gatsby takes down her name, and inside of a week she receives "a package from Croisier's with a new evening gown in it." The volumes in Gatsby's huge, scholarly library are real enough, although a closer look reveals that the pages are uncut; and Nick discovers that even Gatsby's name is slightly fraudulent, only a play on his legal name, "James Gatz."

The true facts of Gatsby's background emerge slowly in the novel, in bits and pieces, as Nick sifts the rumors (and Gatsby's own lies) from the reality of the man, but the fragments add up to a striking portrait of an ambitious young male Promoter. Gatsby's parents were shiftless North Dakota farmers, but the young James Gatz had bolder plans for his life, and "never really accepted them as his parents at all." Even at seventeen, Gatsby longed for wealth and power, pledging his natural Artisan impulse to "the service of a vast, vulgar, and meretricious beauty." He left his modest home, drifting from odd job to odd job, and from woman to woman, "his brown, hardening body" living sensually and contemptuously in what Nick calls Gatsby's "overwhelming self-absorption." But all the while his "heart was in a constant, turbulent riot," believing he was meant for some fabulous success, and absolutely convinced his luck would change.

"An instinct toward his future glory" led him to college in Minnesota, but he stayed only two weeks, "dismayed at [the school's] ferocious indifference to the drums of his destiny." Then by chance Gatsby met his destiny and hired on with Dan Cody, a fifty year old ex-silver miner and multi-millionaire, a Sensualist Artisan sailing his yacht idly around Lake Superior, "a gray, florid man with a hard, empty face—the pioneer debauchee." Cody's yacht represented for Gatsby "all the beauty and glamour in the world," and Cody's lavish, drunken, Dionysian way of life finally satisfied Gatsby's gaudy expectations. James Gatz instantly became the more dashing "Jay Gatsby," and after five years (and three trips around the continent) as everything from Cody's trusted secretary to his male nurse, Gatsby had indeed grown up into a handsome and smoothly manipulative young "gentleman," comfortable with money and power, impulsive and exploitative—having learned quite well, as Nick puts it, "that people liked him when he smiled."

When Dan Cody died, Gatsby was mysteriously swindled out of his inheritance by one of Cody's mistresses, and all Gatsby had to show for his time was a "singularly appropriate education." Poorer but wiser, Gatsby joined the army, and his flamboyant exploits in World War I (leading "two machine-gun detachments so far forward... the infantry couldn't advance") only added to his confidence, validating what he saw as his "enchanted life." After the war and the shower of decorations (and after a few months at Oxford at government expense), Gatsby returned to the states more determined than ever to conquer the world of wealth and success.

Promoters, seemingly burdened with less conscience than many of us, have a natural talent for expediency, almost instinctively knowing the shortest route to their goals; and indeed Gatsby quickly sidestepped the laborious way to the top, taking aim instead at the cutthroat New York underworld. Though he tells Nick "I was in the drug business and then I was in the oil business," his real connections appear to be with big time gamblers and mobsters, and his "chain of drug stores," as Nick eventually finds out, is actually a network of bootleg liquor outlets. Gatsby introduces Nick to his gluttonous mentor in business, Meyer Wolfsheim, the Promoter gambler who fixed the World's Series (and who wears human molars as cuff links), and he casually explains how one could conceive of such an audacious swindle: Wolfsheim toyed with the faith of fifty million people, Gatsby says matter-of-factly, because "He just saw the opportunity." When Nick asks "Why isn't he in jail?" Gatsby answers with the Promoter's arrogant practicality: "They can't get him, old sport. He's a smart man."

Gatsby's own dealings are more obscure in the novel, but appear just as fraudulent. He chats with Wolfsheim about under-the-counter hush money, he takes confidential phone calls from Chicago (Nick overhears one to be about some bond scheme), and when Nick inquires more deeply into the source of his income, Gatsby suspiciously shuts down the conversation: "That's my affair," he quietly insists. Thus, only three years after the Armistice, Gatsby has become the figure of mystery and legend we meet at the beginning of *The Great Gatsby*, a wealthy, suave, and yet somehow sinister young Promoter, seducing a certain glamorous notoriety with his parties, while feeding the lurid imaginations of spongers who only "guessed at his corruption."

There is, of course, one more piece to Gatsby's puzzle, the memory of a lost love, and Nick's somewhat naive belief in the heartfelt sincerity of this romance is the principal reason he overcomes what he calls his "unaffected scorn" for men like Gatsby and tells his story. As before, Nick learns the truth of Gatsby's ill-fated relationship slowly, as the violent events in the novel strip away Gatsby's sophisticated artifices. In the weeks before he left for the war, it appears, Gatsby fell passionately in love with a rich, beautiful, immensely popular young southern debutante named Daisy Fay (greatly resembling Fitzgerald's own wife, Zelda Sayre). Gatsby made love to her in Promoter style—"He took what he could get, ravenously and unscrupulously...under false pretenses"—and then he shipped for France. Daisy (a warmhearted but frivolous Performer Artisan) struggled as best she could to remain faithful to her dashing lieutenant, defied her parents' wishes and wrote Gatsby secretly, but the war, her family's pressure, and Daisy's own impulsiveness conspired to separate them. Finally, after some tears but apparently with some relief, Daisy married Tom Buchanan, another arrogant, competitive Promoter like Gatsby, but this one socially upper crust and already enormously wealthy.

Nick (and certainly Gatsby himself) romanticizes this brief affair into a sacred passion, and such dramatic wishful thinking has misled many readers about Gatsby's real character. Nick admits that Gatsby "had intended, probably, to take what he could and go," but he also believes that by falling in love with Daisy, Gatsby had very nearly devoted himself to a religious quest: he "had committed himself," Nick likens it, "to the following of a grail." And Nick waxes even more poetical (Fitzgerald's one great weakness as a storyteller) in describing what he believes must have been the transfiguring significance of Daisy's first kiss:

> So [Gatsby] waited, listening for a moment longer to the tuning-fork that had been struck upon a star. Then he kissed her. At his lips' touch she blossomed for him like a flower and the incarnation was complete.[6]

Nick may be indulging in a bit of a Pygmalion project himself with Gatsby, convinced that "true love" has transformed the Promoter Artisan into a more faithful Idealist, his own temperament.[7] But Gatsby's own words are less inflated, and certainly truer to the Promoter's impetuous, head over heals style of falling in love:

> I can't describe to you how surprised I was to find out I loved her, old sport. I even hoped for a while that she'd throw me over, but she didn't....Well, there I was, 'way off my ambitions, getting deeper in love every minute, and all of a sudden I didn't care.[8]

Promoters have their romantic side, of course, and certainly Gatsby believes that his one month's affair with

---

[6] F. Scott Fitzgerald, *The Great Gatsby*, p. 112.

[7] Nick's idealizing thus makes him (in literary terms) an "unreliable narrator," even though many critics regard him as a faithful reporter—or as Wayne Booth puts it in *The Rhetoric of Fiction*, "Nick provides thoroughly reliable guidance" (p. 176).

[8] F. Scott Fitzgerald, *The Great Gatsby*, p. 150.

the flower-like "Daisy" was the one miraculous love of his life. And later, during the war, he *is* devastated when he learns of Daisy's marriage, and he eventually returns from Oxford in a wistful search for his lost love, "feeling that if he searched harder, he might have found her."

Fitzgerald (a Performer himself, and quite famous in the twenties for his own romantic posing) may be making his hero too devoted a lover, even losing touch with the Artisan temperament at this point in *The Great Gatsby*.[9] But though Fitzgerald may sentimentalize Gatsby through Nick's eyes, a careful reading of the novel suggests another, more clearly Promoter scenario. Promoters are the masters (rivaled only by the Performers) of the whirlwind courtship, the sudden, irresistible infatuation, and I would argue that Gatsby's love for Daisy is of this impulsive order, and not the conscientious cherishing that Nick wants to believe in. Indeed, Gatsby appears drawn to Daisy, and clings to her memory after the war, less for Daisy's spiritual significance than for her social and economic glamour. Daisy, rich and beautiful and socially important, is not so much an abstract symbol of incorruptible love for Gatsby as she is a concrete embodiment (much like Pygmalion's statue) of the wealth and power he has hungered for all his life.

Gatsby fell in love with Daisy in the first place, as his confession to Nick at the end of the novel makes clear,

---

[9] Fitzgerald admitted in a letter (to John Peale Bishop, dated August 9, 1925) that Gatsby was a "blurred and patchy" character: "I never at any one time saw him clear myself," he went on, "for he started out as one man I knew and then changed into myself."

less because of her value as a person than because of her opulent, upper class way of life. Gatsby assures Nick that he found Daisy "excitingly desirable," but then proceeds to describe in covetous detail Daisy's "rich house" and "her rich, full life." The Fay mansion, he admits, "amazed him—he had never seen such a beautiful house before," the bedrooms "more beautiful and cool than other bedrooms," the corridors promising "gay and radiant activities," and the porches "bright with the bought luxury of starshine." And Daisy's carefree, lavish life, "redolent of orchids and pleasant, cheerful snobbery," and filled with "half a dozen dates a day with half a dozen men," captivated Gatsby, and challenged his competitive, materialistic temperament as well: "It excited him, too, that many men had already loved Daisy—it increased her value in his eyes." Thus Gatsby, a penniless but fiercely ambitious young soldier, saw Daisy less as a young woman to love than as a precious objet d'art to possess, a priceless figurine "gleaming like silver, safe and proud above the hot struggles of the poor," embodying all of his glorious ambitions. And so, although he felt like an imposter in Daisy's fashionable world—or rather *because* "he had no real right to touch her hand"—Gatsby took Daisy's love to prove the greatness of his destiny, almost as a gesture of his own potency.

The war and Tom Buchanan interrupt Gatsby's plans, as I have explained, but he refuses to give up the woman, nor the triumphant, luxurious way of life that, he insists, he felt "married to." Gatsby returns home from the war, then, intent on a grandiose Pygmalion project: first, he will conquer New York society whatever way he can, wringing from it all the splendor rightfully his; and then, through the weight of his money and influence, he will "impress" Daisy (meaning literally "shape her with pressure") into coming back to him. Gatsby wastes little time with the first part of the project, turning to Meyer Wolfsheim and his shady "business gonnegtions" [sic] for help in besting New York. And as soon as he becomes rich enough and imposing enough, he turns his confident and charming Promoter's smile onto Nick Carraway for help in winning back Daisy.

Nick is Daisy's distant cousin, and he knew Tom at Yale before the war, and when Gatsby learns of these connections he approaches Nick with all his manipulative directiveness. Promoters regard nearly everything, including personal relationships, with a utilitarian eye, and Gatsby suddenly befriends Nick for no other reason than to make use of him. Gatsby wants Nick to arrange a private meeting with Daisy (though he conceals much of this at first), and to convince Nick of his trustworthiness Gatsby invites him for lunch in the city, and with a "sideways" glance takes him into his confidence in the car:

> "Look here, old sport," he broke out surprisingly, "what's your opinion of me, anyhow?"
>
> A little overwhelmed, I began the generalized evasions which that question deserves.
>
> "Well, I'm going to tell you something about my life," he interrupted. "I don't want you to get a wrong idea of me from all these stories you hear."
>
> So he was aware of the bizarre accusations that flavored his halls.

> "I'll tell you God's truth." His right hand suddenly ordered divine retribution to stand by.[10]

Promoters (like most other Artisans) will say whatever it takes to get their way, and Gatsby proceeds to witness his life's story for Nick, with "solemn voice" and in "elegant sentences," the truths expertly confused with the lies. He claims that he's from "wealthy people in the Middle West," that he was "educated at Oxford" (a photograph poses him in his blazer with his cricket bat), that he inherited "a good deal of money" when his parents died, that he was an international war hero (he even shows Nick an inscribed medal from "little Montenegro"), and that he lives so ostentatiously now because he's "trying to forget something very sad that...happened to me long ago." Gatsby's "con" here is familiar, attempting to enlist Nick by encouraging his self-esteem, and Nick is indeed impressed at first, flattered by a great man's intimacy. However, some of Gatsby's details ring hollow (when Nick asks "What part of the Middle West?" for example, Gatsby answers "San Francisco"), and Nick can sometimes barely restrain his laughter, while at other times he wonders "if there wasn't something a little sinister about him, after all." In the end, Nick decides that Gatsby's story is too preposterous (and the war medal and the photograph too authentic) to be entirely disbelieved, and he gives himself up at least for the moment to Gatsby's spell: "My incredulity," Nick admits, shaking his head, "was submerged in fascination now." With Nick sufficiently on his side, Gatsby pockets

---

[10] F. Scott Fitzgerald, *The Great Gatsby*, p. 65.

"his souvenirs with satisfaction," and moves in confidently for the sale: "I'm going to make a big request of you today...."

Gatsby thus maneuvers his long-awaited rendezvous with Daisy (Nick agrees to invite her for a mysterious, private tea), and when they face each other after so many years his tactics for reawakening her feelings are entirely characteristic of the Promoter. Keirsey remarks that Artisans in general often express their romantic desires through extravagant gifts and grand gestures,[11] and Gatsby, after a flustered introduction, and then some quieter moments of reminiscence, suddenly decides to show Daisy his mansion. He points out its impressive façade (Promoters are particularly comfortable with façades): "My house looks well, doesn't it?" he demands; "See how the whole front of it catches the light." And he boasts of its impressive inhabitants: "I keep it always full of interesting people, night and day. People who do interesting things. Celebrated people." Gatsby shows Daisy (and Nick as well) through his manicured gardens, his Marie Antoinette music-rooms and Restoration salons, his dressing-rooms and poolrooms and bathrooms, all the while gauging his impact: "He hadn't once ceased looking at Daisy," Nick observes, "and I think he revalued everything in his house according to the measure of response it drew from her." Encouraged by Daisy's admiring silence, Gatsby opens his personal wardrobes holding another layer of his façade, his "massed suits and dressing-gowns and ties"; and then, in an almost Dionysian orgy

---

[11] David Keirsey and Marilyn Bates, *Please Understand Me*, p. 80.

of material wealth, he literally throws his success at Nick and Daisy's feet, much like a painter overwhelming his canvas with a flurry of colors and textures:

> He took out a pile of shirts and began throwing them, one by one, before us, shirts of sheer linen and thick silk and fine flannel, which lost their fold as they fell and covered the table in many-colored disarray. While we admired he brought more and the soft rich heap mounted higher—shirts with stripes and scrolls and plaids in coral and apple-green and lavender and faint orange, with monograms of Indian blue.[12]

Gatsby has the Promoter's instinct for persuasive action, every move almost artistically turned to his advantage, and Daisy (a wealthy Artisan herself) cannot help but surrender to this profligate exhibition of his feelings: "Suddenly, with a strained sound, Daisy bent her head into the shirts and began to cry stormily. 'They're such beautiful shirts,' she sobbed, her voice muffled in the thick folds.'" Daisy's tearful reverence for Gatsby's shirts, even as she bows humbly and immerses herself in their beauty, expresses perfectly the essentially material basis of Artisan love.

In the weeks that follow, Gatsby tries to make up for all the lost years, and yet, even as he takes Daisy away from her husband, Gatsby seems to have something greater than love on his agenda. To Gatsby, Daisy personifies nearly all the Promoter's deepest desires:

---

[12] F. Scott Fitzgerald, *The Great Gatsby*, p. 93.

wealth and social impact, youth and excitement, optimism and victory—at bottom, a belief in his own invincibility. At one point, for example, when Nick is searching for a word to describe Daisy's lovely, musical voice, Gatsby reveals his most honest concern: "Her voice," he explains simply, "is full of money." Again, when Nick cautions Gatsby to let go of the past and love Daisy for herself, Gatsby ignores the power of time with his Promoter's confidence that he can manipulate anything:

> "I wouldn't ask too much of her," I ventured. "You can't repeat the past."
>
> "Can't repeat the past?" he cried incredulously. "Why of course you can!"
>
> He looked around him wildly, as if the past were lurking here in the shadow of his house, just out of reach of his hand.[13]

Let me point out that Gatsby's whole attempt to recapture Daisy's love is not a sentimental "living in the past" or a nostalgic "turning back the clock." As I explained about Meursault, Artisans live largely in the moment, experiencing reality in the present tense, and Gatsby's intention with Daisy is not to cherish the past and nurse it back to life, but to defy the past, to grasp time in his hand and crush it.

Gatsby's Pygmalion ambitions thus cannot be satisfied merely with Daisy's love. Victory is more important to the Promoter than to any other type, and Gatsby's every effort since the war has been devoted to conquering

---

[13] F. Scott Fitzgerald, *The Great Gatsby*, p. 111.

those forces, wealth, social snobbery, marriage vows—even time itself—that denied Gatsby his prize, Daisy, "high in a white palace the king's daughter, the golden girl...." It is not enough, then, for Gatsby merely to win Daisy's love; he must defeat his rival Tom as well, Tom with his money and his breeding and his lawful right to Daisy, and thus erase all those years of frustration and impotence. Promoters hold little sacred in their schemes for revenge (and certainly time means nothing to them), and, indeed, Gatsby believes he can take Tom and Daisy, as well as their years together, and refashion the past to his own vision: "He wanted nothing less of Daisy," Nick concedes, "than that she should go to Tom and say: 'I never loved you.'" And in a final, public confrontation with Tom, as Gatsby presses Daisy with all his interpersonal leverage to verify his words, "Your wife doesn't love you....She's never loved you. She loves me," Nick sees in Gatsby's face the "competitive" cruelty others have remarked: "He looked," Nick confesses reluctantly, "as if he'd 'killed a man.' For a moment the set of his face could be described in just that fantastic way."

Gatsby's enormous effort to bend time and temperament to his will, as many of you know, ends in failure and death. Daisy is a capricious Performer and cannot sustain Gatsby's expectations for long, breaking down finally under the weight of his arrogance: "'Oh, you want too much!' she cried to Gatsby. 'I love you now—isn't that enough? I can't help what's past.'" Daisy's loss of courage (along with Tom's gloating words, "I think he realizes his presumptuous little flirtation is over") confound Gatsby and sober him into confessing much of his real background to Nick, but they never really touch his confidence. All through the final, and somewhat contrived events in the novel (including Daisy running over and killing Tom's mistress with Gatsby's car), Gatsby believes that he will gallantly protect Daisy, win her love, and possess all the power she represents for him. Gatsby is the Promoter at his best throughout these nightmarish last events, coolly balancing on the edge of disaster, expecting each moment to turn defeat into victory—and earning at least Nick's respect for his heroic optimism, what Nick calls his "heightened sensitivity to the promises of life...an extraordinary gift for hope, a romantic readiness such as I have never found in any other person." But Gatsby's extravagant scheme is doomed, and in a last twist of fate, even while "clutching at some last hope" for Daisy, Gatsby is shot to death by the dead mistress's grief-stricken husband.

Nick alone is left to take Gatsby's side and to tell Gatsby's tale, and his final tribute beautifully captures the inherent confidence of the Promoter. At the beginning of the novel, before he knew how to contact Daisy, Gatsby would stroll out at night on his immense lawn, look across the bay, raise his arms and stare at a green "go ahead" port light suspended at the end of Daisy's dock. Nick describes this fascinating scene several times in the novel, the green light (the color of money, by the way) seeming to lure Gatsby on irresistibly, perhaps calling to some essential ambition in his nature. On the last page of *The Great Gatsby*, however, Nick finally understands the meaning of the green light, and his explanation—a last appreciation of Gatsby, really—celebrates the endlessly optimistic Promoter, believing impulsively in his own good fortune, and embracing his inevitable triumph with theatrical flair:

> Gatsby believed in the green light, the orgiastic future that year by year recedes before us. It eluded us then, but that's no matter—tomorrow we will run faster, stretch out our arms farther....And one fine morning—[14]

Becky Sharp

Female Promoter characters rarely receive the romantic coloring that Nick Carraway gives to Gatsby. "Con" women in literature are usually presented much less sympathetically, with the Promoter's inherent craftiness, aggressiveness, and arrogance typically portrayed in women as scheming and willfulness and brazenness. With some notable exceptions (such as Chaucer's dauntless Wife of Bath and Shakespeare's infinitely various Cleopatra), female Promoters are the so-called "bad women" in novels and plays, ruthless social-climbers, conniving mistresses, or cunning, power-hungry matriarchs. Victorian fiction, with its largely black and white morality, and its great new theme of class mobility, abounds with these resourceful, cold-hearted females, making their way in the fashionable world by their wits alone; and the undisputed queen of them all, indeed,

---

[14] F. Scott Fitzgerald, *The Great Gatsby*, p. 182. Textual scholars have discovered that Fitzgerald intended the word "orgiastic" to read "orgasmic," a word with even more Dionysian overtones.

one of the truly unforgettable Promoters in nineteenth century fiction, is Becky Sharp in William Makepeace Thackeray's *Vanity Fair.*

Unlike *The Great Gatsby,* with its fragmented narrative scheme washing time backwards and forwards, collecting the pieces of Gatsby's identity, *Vanity Fair* is a long, straightforward chronicle of Becky Sharp's machinations in love and social warfare, her "Campaign" in Vanity Fair, as Thackeray calls the smug, hypocritical upper layers of English society. Becky begins the novel, indeed, as a "hard-hearted" seventeen year old orphan, tutoring French for her costs at Chiswick Mall, a strict academy for young ladies outside of London. Her parents had both been Artisans, her French mother a music-hall Performer, and her father a Sensualist starving painter:

> He was a clever man; a pleasant companion; a careless student; with a great propensity for running into debt, and a partiality for the tavern. When he was drunk, he used to beat his wife and daughter; and the next morning, with a headache, he would rail at the world for its neglect of his genius.[15]

Despite the mistreatment, father and daughter were inseparable, Becky sitting at his knee, fascinated by "the talk of many of his wild companions" in the artist's quarter in Soho, and delighting the roguish young Bohemians in turn with her precocious wit and her scathing mimicry of respectable ladies. Becky also sharpened her inherent resourcefulness by managing her "lazy,

---

[15] William Makepeace Thackeray, *Vanity Fair,* p. 20.

dissolute, clever, jovial" father's endless line of creditors: "many a tradesman," Thackeray discloses, "had she coaxed and wheedled into good-humour, and into granting one meal more." In contrast with Performers, who seem to play like children all their lives, Promoters seem to have a canniness about them, an adult eye, even when they are children. Thus as a boy, Gatsby spent twice as much time practicing "elocution, poise and how to attain it" as he did playing baseball; and Thackeray tells us that Becky Sharp "had never blushed in her life" and that "she had been a woman since she was eight years old." Although not an innocent herself, Becky knew instinctively how to play "the part of the *ingénue*," and so, when her mother died and then her father died of "his third attack of *delirium tremens*," Becky's show of deference and modesty won her admission at conservative Chiswick, with Thackeray's polite word of condolence for the headmistress: "O why did Miss Pinkerton let such a dangerous bird into her cage?"

Much as Hedda Gabler hated her "tight little world" of Victorian propriety, so Becky, after "the freedom and the beggary of the old studio in Soho," immediately despises the captivity and the predictability of her new Guardian home:

> The rigid formality of the place suffocated her: the prayers and the meals, the lessons and the walks, which were arranged with a conventional regularity, oppressed her almost beyond endurance.[16]

---

[16] William Makepeace Thackeray, *Vanity Fair*, p. 22.

And much as Hedda preferred Judge Brack's risqué friends and conversation, so Becky, after the witty, worldly interplay in her father's Artisan circle, has only contempt for her new companions:

> The pompous vanity of the old schoolmistress, the foolish good-humour of her sister, the silly chat and scandal of the elder girls, and the frigid correctness of the governesses equally annoyed her.[17]

Unlike Hedda's quiet desperation, however, Becky is determined to free herself somehow from this Guardian prison, and so turns from the *ingénue* role that had so charmed Miss Pinkerton and attacks her superior with a shrewd insubordination.

Even at this early age Becky knows how to infuriate as well as to flatter her opponent,[18] and as she laughs sarcastically in Miss Pinkerton's pinched face, she very nearly sends "the school-mistress into fits." Then, when Miss Pinkerton attempts to scold her in public, Becky hits upon a wonderfully wicked "plan of answering her in French," a language the old woman only pretends to know. This is an inspired bit of gamesmanship, and suggests how cool under fire Becky can be. Answering

---

[17] William Makepeace Thackeray, *Vanity Fair*, p. 22.

[18] David S. Janowsky, et al., "Playing the Manic Game," *Archives of General Psychiatry*, Vol. 22, March, 1970, pp. 253-254. Dr. Janowsky and his associates describe how, after building another's self-esteem, "the manic patient may reverse his stance, taking away as well as giving, and making another feel demeaned and degraded" (p. 254).

Miss Pinkerton's rage with polite French not only reminds the headmistress of her deficiencies in education (thus belittling her administrative function in the school), but it also proves Becky the superior scholar, and leaves her blameless in the interaction. In one brilliant move, Becky demurely feigns respect and mocks Miss Pinkerton to her face. Miss Pinkerton (tall and stiff and turbanned) is a formidable enemy, having "done battle" against her students for years, but such elegant tactics, Thackeray admits, "quite routed the old woman," and she hurriedly places Becky as a governess for a private family.

Thus launched into the world, Becky (now nineteen) surveys her immediate future with her Promoter's fearless, practical eye. She knows she's "alone in the world," with "only herself and her own wits to trust to," but she rises boldly to the challenge: "Well," she muses, almost eager to commence, "let us see if my wits cannot provide me with an honourable maintenance." Becky Sharp is a memorable creation because her behavior is so thoroughly tactical; Thackeray excuses her at times (half-heartedly), and apologizes for her on occasion (ironically), but most often he analyzes her maneuvers with accuracy and amusement. "What a sly little devil! what a little fox," one character, "chuckling with pleasure," calls Becky, and it seems Thackeray would agree.

Becky's first objective is to secure as quickly as possible the most acceptable means of maintenance for a nineteenth century female—a husband. Indeed, she makes a play, sight unseen, for the first wealthy, unattached bachelor she encounters in the novel, one Jos (Joseph)

Sedley, the older brother of Amelia Sedley, her only friend from Chiswick, and Thackeray allows that Becky's "first move showed considerable skill." Becky's most effective tactic for handling people is "to make herself, as she said, agreeable to her benefactors, and to gain their confidence to the utmost of her power," and though the young man turns out to be an obese, peevish, and insufferably vain Guardian, Becky perseveres, laughing cordially at his jokes, complimenting him to his mother just loudly enough to be overheard, doting tearfully on his sister, and in short feigning every regard she can to extract "the interesting avowal from the bashful lips of the young man." As he does so often in *Vanity Fair*, Thackeray compliments her pluck and dexterity: "If Miss Rebecca can get the better of *him*, and at her first entrance into life, she is a young person of no ordinary cleverness." But Becky's career in duplicity has just begun, and Fate (as well as the admiring Novelist) intervenes on her behalf, chasing Jos back to India in embarrassed retreat, and saving Becky from such a waste of her talents.

As a Promoter, Becky is quite comfortable with revenge ("Revenge may be wicked," she believes, "but it's natural"), and her attitude toward her "little misadventure" with Jos is a mixture of resentment and retaliation:

> I am alone in the world....I have nothing to look for but what my own labour can bring me; and while that little pink-faced chit Amelia, with not half my sense, has ten thousand pounds and an establishment secure....Well, let us see...if some day or the other I cannot

> show Miss Amelia my real superiority over her...it will be a fine day when I can take my place above her in the world, as why, indeed, should I not?[19]

To begin elevating her place in the world, then, Becky sets her sights on the family, and the fortune, of Sir Pitt Crawley, the Baronet for whose family she has become governess. Becky's tactics are, once again, surreptitious: she resolves "to make friends of every one around her who could at all interfere with her comfort" (the phrase "make friends" drips with irony). Working quickly, she wins over the children by turning their instruction into play, and she cultivates the good will of Lady Crawley by showing her a "cool respect." But her real effort is with the men of the family. With old Sir Pitt (a crusty, parsimonious Guardian), she is so attentive to his estate business and to his endless lawsuits that she "quite [wins] the Baronet's confidence," and soon becomes virtual mistress of place, writing his letters, managing his accounts, though shrewdly keeping a "modest and affable" profile with the other servants. With the elder son, Mr. Pitt (another Guardian, stern and fastidious), Becky compliments his learning, admires his prudent taste, and "was often affected, even to tears" by his tedious evening discourses on politics and religion. And finally, with the younger son, Captain Rawdon Crawley (a charming, rakish young Performer), Becky makes the most impressive moves of all: she fascinates him by boldly puffing on his cigar and fearlessly riding his kicking

---

[19] William Makepeace Thackeray, *Vanity Fair*, p. 88.

mare; she keeps him at arm's length by modestly parrying his public flirtations; and while the family is thus kept off balance, she marries him secretly.

Becky's conquest and disposition of these three Crawley men occupy much of her time in *Vanity Fair*, and provide quite a comprehensive look at the cynical side of Promoter love. First of all, when Lady Crawley suddenly dies, old Sir Pitt even more suddenly asks Becky to marry him, and his proposal reveals just how deeply Becky's Dionysian charm has affected the stingy Guardian:

> "I'll make you happy, zee if I don't. You shall do what you like; spend what you like; and 'av it all your own way"...and the old man fell down on his knees and leered at her like a satyr.[20]

Becky melodramatically declines the offer, confessing to Sir Pitt that she's already married, and weeping "some of the most genuine tears that ever fell from her eyes." Later, however, alone and recovering her wits, she indulges in what Thackeray amusedly terms some "sincere and touching regrets" at having missed such a chance, and her Promoter's imagination toys with the wealth and social impact she might have commanded:

> Rebecca thought to herself, in all the woes of repentance—and I might have been my lady! I might have led that old man whither I would... I might have had the townhouse newly furnished and decorated. I would have had the

[20] William Makepeace Thackeray, *Vanity Fair*, p. 142.

> handsomest carriage in London, and a box at the Opera; and I would have been presented next season. All this *might* have been.[21]

Promoters waste little time on anything so abstract and idle as regret, however, and indeed Becky permits herself only these few moments of "useless and unseemly sorrow for the irrevocable past." The moment at hand is the natural time-frame of all the Artisans, and what to do next is their immediate concern, and so Becky, like a general determined to get on with the campaign, "wisely turned her whole attention towards the future, which was now vastly more important to her. And she surveyed her position, and its hopes, doubts, and chances."

Becky's attentions to the younger Pitt Crawley suffer a long interruption at this point, as the "artful little hussy" (as she is now openly called) and her dashing but penniless husband become persona non grata with the Crawley family. But the seeds of flattery Becky sowed in those first years as governess grow to harvest later in the novel. After old Sir Pitt dies, Becky maneuvers a reconciliation with the new Sir Pitt and his wife, Lady Jane Sheepshanks (yes, like "Sharp" and "Pitt Crawley," many of Thackeray's names depict character). Becky's approach is still to make "as many friends...as she could possibly bring under control," and so she "artlessly" embraces Lady Jane, feigns a motherly interest in her "dear little children," and with Sir Pitt, "She doubled the deference which before had charmed him." Becky's private agenda has always been for her own husband to inherit the

---

[21] William Makepeace Thackeray, *Vanity Fair*, p. 148.

Crawley property and title: "Even now," she tells herself, patiently, "there was only that puling, sickly Pitt Crawley between Rawdon and a baronetcy; and should anything happen to the former, all would be well." But in lieu of such good fortune, she "prosecutes," as Thackeray calls it, other "schemes and hopes" for Sir Pitt:

> Rebecca listened to Pitt, she talked to him, she sang to him, she coaxed him, and cuddled him, so that...he thought to himself how she respected him and how he deserved it, and how...mum and stupid his own wife was compared to that brilliant little Becky.[22]

Though infidelity is certainly not beneath her (indeed, she becomes the wealthy Lord Steyne's mistress by the end of the novel), Becky's intention with Sir Pitt, almost a casual Pygmalion project, is purely pecuniary. She and Rawdon desperately need money, and if she can turn the frigid, bookish Guardian even a little into a more aggressive and impulsive Artisan like herself, she may loosen up his checkbook. And so, in true Promoter style, she prods Pitt's ambition and convinces him of his "commanding talents":

> No, Sir Pitt Crawley, I know you better...I know what you want. You want to distinguish yourself in Parliament; everyone says you are the finest speaker in England....And you want to be Baron Crawley of Queen's Crawley, and you will before you die. I saw it all. I could read your heart.[23]

---

[22] William Makepeace Thackeray, *Vanity Fair*, p. 427.

[23] William Makepeace Thackeray, *Vanity Fair*, pp. 437-438.

Acting almost like a carnival fortune-teller, Becky mesmerizes her victim, fully "taking in" Sir Pitt (literally "entrancing" him) with the depth of her insight: "Pitt Crawley was amazed and enraptured with her speech. 'How that woman comprehends me!' he said." Of course, as Keirsey points out,[24] Promoters only appear to comprehend others with such uncanny intuition; in truth, they know (or "con") their victims' deepest wishes through their innately acute powers of observation—as Becky herself sums up the Artisan's sensitivity: "I saw it all." Whatever the source of Becky's insight, however, the effect on Sir Pitt is indeed amazing. Not only does he open up his house—and, reluctantly, his pocketbook—to Becky and Rawdon, but he also becomes a newly hospitable and popular magnate in his borough, dining out liberally, attending county balls, and even playing whist with the Venerable Archdeacon. Never were Becky's self-centered manipulations more happily concluded.

Becky's more ambitious Pygmalion project, however, is with her husband, and it is a far less successful affair. Even during their clandestine courtship (what Becky later calls "my promotion") she had her Promoter's eye on what she could make of Captain Rawdon Crawley. "Rawdy" is an archetypal Performer, "a celebrated 'blood,' or dandy about town," reckless, loud, impetuous, liberal with his money and his liquor, the darling of the ladies and the valorous leader of his regiment of dragoons. Becky is clearly charmed by this large, frisky puppy of a man (who is very much like her father), but without

---

[24] David Keirsey and Marilyn Bates, *Please Understand Me*, p. 196.

question she marries Rawdon to turn him into a fox like herself. Rawdon is the pampered favorite of his rich spinster aunt, old Miss Crawley, herself a radical old *bel esprit* Performer, and Becky's intention throughout the first half of the novel is to "come round" the old girl's fortune if only Rawdon will be clever and help. "Dearest!" she urges Rawdon, to give him confidence,

> something *tells me* we shall conquer. You shall leave that odious regiment: quit gaming, racing, and *be a good boy*; and we shall live in Park Lane, and *ma tante* shall leave us all her money.[25]

But to complicate matters, old Miss Crawley feels betrayed when she learns of Rawdon's marriage, and disowns the young man in a rage, forcing Becky to push her good-natured husband all the harder to bring his aunt around: "Becky told him...the time for action had arrived," and Rawdon "expressed himself as ready to act under her orders, as he would be to charge with his troop at the command of his colonel." Like most Promoters in such a crisis, Becky's "nerves seemed to be of iron," and when the more kindly Rawdon loses heart a bit, wondering, "Suppose the old lady doesn't come to?" Becky assures him, "*I'll* make your fortune."

As we have seen so often with would-be Pygmalions, however, Becky's "project" (as she calls it herself) for her husband fails from the very start. Rawdon is far too easygoing and playful ever to join effectively in her manipulations. He is quite happy living as richly as

---

[25] William Makepeace Thackeray, *Vanity Fair*, pp. 149-150.

Becky can manage for him "on nothing a-year," piling up huge debts on food and entertainment, and staying one step ahead of his creditors. Indeed, while Becky outwits the credit lawyers in the "most difficult negotiations," Rawdon plays the gentlemanly dragoon, with everything "plentiful in his house but ready money." As a Performer, his ambition in the marriage is to have a good time, not to assault and conquer Vanity Fair, and thus, as old Miss Crawley remains unforgiving, Becky's hopes for wealth and social power slowly turn to bitter recriminations. She begins to see Rawdon's lightheartedness as soft and stupid: "If he had but a little more brains," she says to herself, "I might make something of him." And though she rarely lets Rawdon see her contempt for him, she soon regards him as little more than a mischievous child, calling him "Goosey," ordering him condescendingly to "be a good boy, and obey your schoolmistress," and taking full advantage of his simplicity and affection:

> She did not even show her scorn much for him; perhaps she liked him better for being a fool. He was her upper servant and *maître d'hotel*. He went on her errands; obeyed her orders without question; took her to the Opera-box; solaced himself at his club during the performance, and came punctually back to fetch her when due.[26]

Becky may be disappointed with her husband's lack of aggressiveness, but she maintains the appearance of optimism even as she ridicules him: "Why, my stupid love," she promises Rawdon, "we have not done with

---

[26] William Makepeace Thackeray, *Vanity Fair*, p. 370.

your aunt yet"; and later, when old Miss Crawley dies and leaves all her money to Mr. Pitt, Becky shrugs off Rawdon's fears for their future with all her Promoter's confidence:

> Ruined! fiddlededee! I will get you a good place before that; or, Pitt and his little boy will die, and we will be Sir Rawdon and my lady. While there is life, there is hope, my dear, and I intend to make a man of you yet.[27]

Like so many of Becky's promises, however, this one is hollow, made more for effect than out of commitment. In truth, though she is fond of Rawdon, she is bored and irritated by his kindness, his lap-dog attentiveness, and she quietly distances herself from him, and from their son. Becky is more excited "thinking about her position or her pleasures or her advancement in society," and she soon turns her talents even more shrewdly to the conquest of Vanity Fair, estranging herself, almost by design, from her family.[28]

In her hard-edged, practical virtuosity with concrete reality, Becky is, like all the Artisans, "an artist herself, as she said very truly," only hers is the art of manipulating people, shaping them to her purpose, convincing them to believe in her even as she picks their pockets. And in the second half of the novel, as she scrounges and chisels

---

[27] William Makepeace Thackeray, *Vanity Fair*, p. 363.

[28] David S. Janowsky, et al., "Playing the Manic Game," *Archives of General Psychiatry*, Vol. 22, March, 1970, pp. 257-259. The article details the manic's (the Artisan's) "characteristic maneuvers which distance him from his family" (p. 257).

her way into the center of the greatest circles of London fashion, she inspires the same sort of mysterious legend that Gatsby heard whispered at his parties, an uneasy mixture of admiration and contempt: Becky, the consummate Promoter,

> provoked, or disarmed, or amused [the] lookers-on, as the case might be. "How cool that woman is," said one; "what airs of independence she assumes"..."What an honest and good-natured soul she is," said another. "What an artful little minx," said a third. They were all right very likely; but Becky went her own way, and so fascinated the professional personages.[29]

Victorian public morality was too conventional, of course, to let Becky prosper for very long, no matter how much Thackeray admired her impertinence. Vanity Fair (no matter how hypocritically) demands Christian justice in its novels—or, as Oscar Wilde was to put it some fifty years later: "The good end happily, and the bad unhappily. That is what fiction means."[30] And so, to satisfy the professional personages, Thackeray sees to it that Rawdon discovers Becky's affair with Lord Steyne (pronounced, significantly, as "stain"), and the ensuing scandal banishes her to the continent. Becky makes the best of her catastrophe, circulating among the fashionable resorts—"From Boulogne to Dieppe, from Dieppe to Caen, from Caen to Tours"—trying with all her arts to appear respectable, playing the "mistreated wife" and the

---

[29] William Makepeace Thackeray, *Vanity Fair*, p. 488.

[30] Oscar Wilde, *The Importance of Being Earnest*, p. 58.

"deprived mother." Thackeray tells us "Becky loved society, and...could no more exist without it than an opium-eater without his dram," but Promoters tire rather quickly of propriety, and indeed, for Becky, "the life of humdrum virtue grew utterly tedious." Searching for excitement, she begins to rouge her face immodestly, to enjoy her cognac and water excessively, and to gamble "audaciously" at the *écarté* tables. And as her money and her reputation dwindle even further, her life comes full circle, back to the Bohemian Artisan existence of her childhood. She has a "wild, roving nature, inherited from father and mother," Thackeray reminds us, and after a series of infamous adventures, she finally settles in a ramshackle garret among "pedlars, punters, tumblers, students and all." Thackeray never loses sight of her Promoter's optimism, however, and—despite her reduced circumstances—Becky insists she "was not worse now than...in the days of her prosperity—only a little down on her luck." Indeed, to the last page of the novel she never once ceases "her intrigues" to recover her losses, leaving the lords and ladies of Vanity fair to wonder nervously, "the little minx, has she come to light again?"

* * * * *

Let me be clear: few Promoters are as ruthless in their subterfuges as Becky Sharp, or as callous in their personal interactions; but without question, the Promoters are the most enterprising Pygmalions of all the Artisans, and share in some measure Becky's opportunistic nature. While the Sensualists and the Performers prefer seduction to coercion, and the Instrumentalists are usually more skillful wielding tools than people, the Promoters see much of life as a negotiation or a sales campaign, and can regard even their loved ones as "marks" to be convinced, connived, or simply "conned" into fascinated compliance. Promoters are also the most guileful of all the Artisans, quite comfortable saying whatever needs to be said, or adopting whatever attitude is necessary to get their way in a relationship. Lovers of other type often have a hard time knowing who they are dealing with, or how to assess their security—they're usually having a sensational time with a Promoter, but are not quite sure who they've fallen in love with. Thus, in loving a Promoter, our wisest course is not to demand too much security or authenticity from them, nor to expect much other than material success to be sacred; we must learn to hold our breath and enjoy their fast ride, overlooking their sometimes distressing lack of conscience (Promoters *really don't* mind taking advantage of people), but also appreciating their amazing confidence and their indomitable entrepreneurship.

Afterword

> *'Tis time; descend; be stone no more; approach;*
> *Strike all that look upon with marvel. Come...*
> *Dear life redeems you.*
>
> —William Shakespeare[1]

The nearly dozen characters I've described as Artisans in this volume are all extreme personalities—two (Meursault and Hedda Gabler) even arguably insane. This book is not about the many happily-adjusted Artisans who go about their lives with humor and with patience, and who find successful marriages and friendships. Literature rarely concerns itself very deeply with ordinary, healthy relationships; drama by its very nature springs from conflict—protagonist requires antagonist—and literature is at its best when examining the exceptional character or the breakdown of harmonious relations. In *Hamlet*, for example, we barely hear of Hamlet's unclouded youth in the peaceful court at Elsinore; the action begins only after Hamlet's uncle and his mother (both Operator Artisans, by the way) poison his father

---

[1] William Shakespeare, *The Winter's Tale*, V,iii,99-103.

and spread the royal bed with incestuous sheets. This may suggest that the mirror of fiction only distorts reality, forcing its characters into twisted predicaments; but from another point of view, fiction may be seen to intensify reality—to magnify it in a sense—by putting its characters under extraordinary tensions and then observing their archetypal reactions. The resulting clarification of character often delights us with its accuracy, but it may also disturb us with its honesty: indeed, this is the intrinsic power of fiction, to charm us as well as to unsettle us into new awareness—not of what is commonplace, but what is characteristic.

Again, clearly, the characters I've discussed are not ordinary human beings, and yet I hope—precisely *because* they are larger-than-life—that they have shed some new light on the Artisans' instinctive patterns of thought and behavior. As a whole, the characters show the Artisans to be born lovers, skillful, entertaining, spontaneous, physically sensitive, sexually stimulating—the natural artists of intimate relations. And indeed, in the right relationships, when allowed their freedom and appreciated for their virtuosity, they make fascinating love partners, particularly for the Guardians (who share their concrete sense of the world), but also for the more abstract Rationals and Idealists. However, like us all, the Artisans have a darker side, and my examples from literature show that in the wrong relationships Artisans can become quite coercive in their interactions. Player Artisans seem naturally reluctant to start up Pygmalion projects (and would prefer to escape such infighting), but in constraining relationships, pressed too hard by a disappointed loved one, they will retaliate with fierce and frequently self-destructive manipulation. Operator Artisans appear more ambitious in their Pygmalion projects—more confident in using people, and even more comfortable with revenge—though they, too, would rather live and let live in their relationships, and resort to desperate tactics only in situations of extraordinary repression.

But what the mirror of fiction clarifies most about the Artisans, I believe, is how consistently the other temperaments misunderstand and mistreat them. The dutiful Guardians, for example, look at the Artisans' impetuosity and unconscious ease with life—their essential mischievousness—and see at times a lack of moral fiber. The literature suggests that the Artisans, living happily in the moment, and with a practical sense of morality, are simply burdened with less conscience than the Guardians find acceptable in their loved ones—and so they take up Pygmalion projects to pound some responsibility into what they regard as wayward souls.

The Idealists, on the other hand, look at the Artisans' unconscious ease with the external forms of life—their instinctive oneness with nature and with art—and often see unspoken profundity. The literature suggests that the Artisans, at home in the physical, concrete world of *things*, gifted with their hands and their tools, simply think less philosophically about the world—have less abstract imagination—than the Idealists believe is possible in their loved ones. Indeed (and this can be a troubling irony for the Idealists), the Artisans' amazing facility in art may derive directly from their freedom from the tangles of a more abstract consciousness. Artisans don't *think* much about their art, they just do it. But the Idealists want their art—and their artists—to be meaningful and deep, and so they mount Pygmalion projects to invest the Artisans with wisdom and a poetic introspection.

And, finally, the one Rational character I discuss looks at the Artisans' absence of forethought—their incurable impulsiveness—and sees an aimlessness of mind, or perhaps even a lack of intelligence. After berating Norman for his philandering, Ruth relents a bit and reveals her real attitude: Norman is not actually contemptible, "just stupid....You just don't think." *The Norman Conquests* suggests that, indeed, Artisans simply *don't* think much beyond the task (or the person) at hand—theirs is tactical intelligence, not strategical, like the Rationals'. And so Ruth admits that her Pygmalion project to shape up Norman's spur of the moment mind—"to try and make [Norman] behave like a husband"—has failed.

The implication of these fictional portraits is thus clear, if perhaps too colorfully drawn: the Artisans are not immoral, or superficial, or mindless for being so impulsive in their lives; they are simply different in fundamental—and invaluable—ways from the rest of us. If we all (including the Artisans) will put down our hammers and chisels, and respect the gifts that each temperament is blessed with—and that we cannot change in any event—we can redeem our relationships, turning our hardened, embattled statues once again into loving partners.

Appendix A

A Note on Artisan Poetry

English and American poetry after World War I, rejecting the lofty sentiment and the formal, flowery diction of late Victorian and Edwardian poetry, took as one of its major objectives the need to speak plainly about concrete reality. Ezra Pound's warning "Go in fear of abstractions" was the founding creed of the movement known as "Imagist" poetry, while William Carlos Williams became the central voice in a school of poetry aptly named "Objectivist." Other influential poets of the time, while not associating themselves with a particular movement, embraced this objective whole-heartedly. Archibald MacLeish defined this new poetry in "Ars Poetica" (1926), asserting paradoxically that "A poem should be wordless/ As the flight of birds," and concluding, "A poem should not mean/But be." And Wallace Stevens played with this sense of the concrete all through his poetry; he insisted "Let be be finale of seem," in "The Emperor of Ice-Cream" (1921); he made the ultimate reduction of diction in "The Man on the Dump" (1938), trying to express the concrete essence of a "thing" with the minimalist phrase, "The the"; and late in his career he entitled poems "The

Plain Sense of Things" (1951) and "Not Ideas About the Thing but the Thing Itself" (1954).

Many readers find this kind of modern poetry difficult because they have trouble finding comprehensible meanings in the poems. Readers even call such poems "obscure" or "abstract" because they have trouble grasping their intellectual message. If anything, however, these poems are concrete, insisting that they have no meaning beyond the concrete things they describe; and thus the difficulty lies not in the poems but in the conscientious reader's inability to give up his or her need for abstraction. This is the problem, for example, with a simple poem such as Williams's famous and seemingly enigmatic "The Red Wheelbarrow":

> so much depends
> upon
>
> a red wheel
> barrow
>
> glazed with rain
> water
>
> beside the white
> chickens.

In other words, so much of the beauty and contentment in our lives depends upon the sensual, concrete—the Artisan—things we have lost touch with in our complicated and abstracted existence.

Appendix B

The Keirsey Temperament Sorter

Please use the answer sheet on page 165.

1. **At a party do you**
   (a) interact with many, including strangers
   (b) interact with a few, known to you
2. **Are you more**
   (a) realistic than speculative
   (b) speculative than realistic
3. **Is it worse to**
   (a) have your "head in the clouds"
   (b) be "in a rut"
4. **Are you more drawn toward the**
   (a) convincing (b) emotions
5. **Are you more drawn toward the**
   (a) convincing (b) touching
6. **Do you prefer to work**
   (a) to deadlines (b) just "whenever"
7. **Do you tend to choose**
   (a) rather carefully
   (b) somewhat impulsively
8. **At parties do you**
   (a) stay late, with increasing energy
   (b) leave early, with decreased energy

9. **Are you more attracted to**
   (a) what is actual (b) what is possible
10. **Are you more interested in**
    (a) sensible people (b) imaginative people
11. **In judging others are you more swayed by**
    (a) laws than circumstances
    (b) circumstances than laws
12. **In approaching others is your indication to be somewhat**
    (a) objective (b) personal
13. **Are you more**
    (a) punctual (b) leisurely
14. **Does it bother you more having things**
    (a) incomplete (b) completed
15. **In your social groups do you**
    (a) keep abreast of other's happenings
    (b) get behind on the news
16. **In doing ordinary things are you more likely to**
    (a) do it the usual way (b) do it your own way
17. **Writers should**
    (a) "say what they mean and mean what they say"
    (b) express things more by use of analogy
18. **Which appeals to you more**
    (a) consistency of thought
    (b) harmonious human relationships
19. **Are you more comfortable in making**
    (a) logical judgments (b) value judgments
20. **Do you want things**
    (a) settled and decided
    (b) unsettled and undecided
21. **Would you say you are more**
    (a) serious and determined (b) easy-going

22. In phoning do you
(a) rarely question that it will all be said
(b) rehearse what you'll say

23. Facts
(a) "speak for themselves" (b) illustrate principles

24. Are visionaries
(a) somewhat annoying (b) rather fascinating

25. Are you more often
(a) a cool-headed person
(b) a warm-hearted person

26. Is it worse to be
(a) unjust (b) merciless

27. Should one usually let events occur
(a) by careful selection and choice
(b) randomly and by chance

28. Do you feel better about
(a) having purchased
(b) having the option to buy

29. In company do you
(a) initiate conversation
(b) wait to be approached

30. Common sense is
(a) rarely questionable
(b) frequently questionable

31. Children often do not
(a) make themselves useful enough
(b) exercise their fantasy enough

32. In making decisions do you feel more comfortable with
(a) standards (b) feelings

33. Are you more
(a) firm than gentle (b) gentle than firm

34. Which is more admirable:
(a) the ability to organize and be methodical
(b) the ability to adapt and make do

35. Do you put more value on the
(a) definite (b) open-ended

36. Does new and non-routine interaction with others
(a) stimulate and energize you
(b) tax your reserves

37. Are you more frequently
(a) a practical sort of person
(b) a fanciful sort of person

38. Are you more likely to
(a) see how others are useful
(b) see how others see

39. Which is more satisfying:
(a) to discuss an issue thoroughly
(b) to arrive at agreement on an issue

40. Which rules you more:
(a) your head (b) your heart

41. Are you more comfortable with work that is
(a) contracted
(b) done on a casual basis

42. Do you tend to look for
(a) the orderly (b) whatever turns up

43. Do you prefer
(a) many friends with brief contact
(b) a few friends with more lengthy contact

44. Do you go more by
(a) facts (b) principles

45. Are you more interested in
(a) production and distribution
(b) design and research

46. Which is more of a compliment:
(a) "There is a very logical person."
(b) "There is a very sentimental person."

47. Do you value in yourself more that you are
(a) unwavering (b) devoted

48. Do you more often prefer the
(a) final and unalterable statement
(b) tentative and preliminary statement

49. Are you more comfortable
(a) after a decision (b) before a decision

50. Do you
(a) speak easily and at length with strangers
(b) find little to say to strangers

51. Are you more likely to trust your
(a) experience (b) hunch

52. Do you feel
(a) more practical than ingenious
(b) more ingenious than practical

53. Which person is more to be complimented: one of
(a) clear reason (b) strong feeling

54. Are you inclined more to be
(a) fair-minded (b) sympathetic

55. Is it preferable mostly to
(a) make sure things are arranged
(b) just let things happen

56. In relationships should most things be
(a) renegotiable
(b) random and circumstantial

57. When the phone rings do you
(a) hasten to get to it first
(b) hope someone else will answer

58. Do you prize more in yourself
(a) a strong sense of reality (b) a vivid imagination

59. Are you drawn more to
(a) fundamentals (b) overtones

60. Which seems the greater error:
(a) to be too passionate (b) to be too objective

61. Do you see yourself as basically
(a) hard-headed (b) soft-hearted

62. Which situation appeals to you more:
(a) the structural and scheduled
(b) the unstructured and unscheduled

63. Are you a person that is more
(a) routinized than whimsical
(b) whimsical than routinized

64. Are you more inclined to be
(a) easy to approach (b) somewhat reserved

65. In writings do you prefer
(a) the more literal (b) the more figurative

66. Is it harder for you to
(a) identify with others (b) utilize others

67. Which do you wish more for yourself:
(a) clarity of reason
(b) strength of compassion

68. Which is the greater fault:
(a) being indiscriminate (b) being critical

69. Do you prefer the
(a) planned event (b) unplanned event

70. Do you tend to be more
(a) deliberate than spontaneous
(b) spontaneous than deliberate

Answer Sheet

Enter a check for each answer in the column for **a** or **b**.

	A	B		A	B		A	B		A	B		A	B		A	B		A	B
1			2			3			4			5			6			7		
8			9			10			11			12			13			14		
15			16			17			18			19			20			21		
22			23			24			25			26			27			28		
29			30			31			32			33			34			35		
36			37			38			39			40			41			42		
43			44			45			46			47			48			49		
50			51			52			53			54			55			56		
57			58			59			60			61			62			63		
64			65			66			67			68			69			70		
1			2 3			4 3			4 5			6 5			6 7			8 7		8

1			2	3			4	5			6	7			8
	E	**I**			**S**	**N**			**T**	**F**			**J**	**P**	

Directions for Scoring

1. **Add down** so that the total number of "a" answers is written in the box at the bottom of each column (see next page for illustration). Do the same for the "b" answers you have checked. Each of the 14 boxes should have a number in it.

2. **Transfer the number** in box No. 1 of the answer sheet to box No. 1 below the answer sheet. Do this for box No. 2 as well. Note, however, that you have two numbers for boxes 3 through 8. Bring down the first number for each box beneath the second, as indicated by the arrows. Now add all the pairs of numbers and enter the total in the boxes below the answer sheet, so each box has only one number.

3. **Now you have** four pairs of numbers. Circle the letter below the larger number of each pair (see answer sheet on the next page for illustration). If the two numbers of any pair are equal, then circle neither, but put a large X below them and circle it.

You have now identified your "type." It should be one of the following:

INFP	**ISFP**	**INTP**	**ISTP**
ENFP	**ESFP**	**ENTP**	**ESTP**
INFJ	**ISFJ**	**INTJ**	**ISTJ**
ENFJ	**ESFJ**	**ENTJ**	**ESTJ**

Sample Answer Sheet

See "Directions for Scoring" on the facing page.

	A	B		A	B		A	B		A	B		A	B		A	B		A	B
1	X		2	X		3	X		4		X	5		X	6	X		7		X
8	X		9	X		10	X		11		X	12		X	13	X		14	X	
15	X		16	X		17	X		18		X	19		X	20	X		21	X	
22		X	23	X		24	X		25		X	26		X	27	X		28	X	
29	X		30	X		31		X	32		X	33		X	34	X		35	X	
36	X		37	X		38	X		39		X	40		X	41	X		42	X	
43		X	44		X	45	X		46		X	47		X	48	X		49		X
50	X		51	X		52	X		53		X	54	X		55	X		56	X	
57	X		58	X		59	X		60		X	61		X	62	X		63		X
64	X		65	X		66		X	67		X	68		X	69	X		70	X	
1	*8*	*2*	2 3	*9*	*1*	4 3	*8*	*2*	4 5	*0*	*10*	6 5	*1*	*9*	6 7	*10*	*0*	8 7	*7*	*3*
							9	*1*					*0*	*10*					*10*	*0*

(last column group: 8)

1			2	3			4	5			6	7			8
	8	*2*			*17*	*3*			*1*	*19*			*17*	*3*	
	(E)	I			(S)	N			T	(F)			(J)	P	

If you have an X in your type, yours is a mixed type. An X can show up in any of the four pairs: E or I, S or N, T or F, and J or P. Hence there are 32 mixed types besides the 16 listed above:

XNTP	**EXTP**	**ENXP**	**ENTX**
XNTJ	**EXTJ**	**INXP**	**INTX**
XNFP	**EXFP**	**ENXJ**	**ENFX**
XNFJ	**EXFJ**	**INXJ**	**INFX**
XSTP	**IXTP**	**ESXP**	**ESTX**
XSTJ	**IXTJ**	**ISXP**	**ISTX**
XSFP	**IXFP**	**ESXJ**	**ESFX**
XSFJ	**IXFJ**	**ISXJ**	**ISFX**

You will find a description of your type in *Please Understand Me* by David Keirsey and Marilyn Bates, and more detailed discussion in *Portraits of Temperament* by David Keirsey. If you have an X in your type, yours is a combination of two types. If, for example, the E and I scores are equal and the type is, say, XSFJ, then you would read both ESFJ and ISFJ portraits and decide for yourself which parts of each description are applicable.

Bibliography

Albee, Edward. *Who's Afraid of Virginia Woolf?* New York: Atheneum, 1981.

Austen, Jane. *Pride and Prejudice.* New York: Bantam Books, 1981.

Ayckbourn, Alan. *The Norman Conquests.* New York: Grove Press, Inc., 1979.

Booth, Wayne C. *The Rhetoric of Fiction.* Chicago & London: The University of Chicago Press, 1961.

Camus, Albert. *The Stranger.* Trans. Stuart Gilbert. New York: Random House, 1954.

Cary, Joyce. *The Horse's Mouth.* New York: Harper & Row, 1965.

Chaucer, Geoffrey. *The Canterbury Tales.* Trans. Nevill Coghill. New York: Penguin Books, 1977.

Cleckley, Hervey. *The Mask of Sanity.* Saint Louis: The C.V. Mosby Company, 1964.

Cohen, B. Bernard. *Writing About Literature.* Glenview, Illinois: Scott, Foresman and Company, 1973.

Durrell, Lawrence. *Justine.* New York: E.P. Dutton & Co., Inc., 1960.

Euripides. *The Bacchae*. Trans. William Arrowsmith. In Grene, David, and Richmond Lattimore, eds. *Greek Tragedies, Volume 3*. Chicago & London: The University of Chicago Press, 1965.

Fielding, Henry. *Tom Jones*. New York: W.W. Norton & Company, Inc. 1973.

Fitzgerald, F. Scott. *The Great Gatsby*. New York: Charles Scribner's Sons, 1953.

________. *The Crack-Up*. Ed. Edmund Wilson. New York: New Directions Publishing Corp., 1956.

Flint, F.S., and Ezra Pound. "Imagisme." *Poetry*, I, (1913), 198-206.

Forster, E.M. *Aspects of the Novel*. New York: Harcourt, Brace & World, 1954.

Fowles, John. *The Ebony Tower*. New York and Toronto: New American Library, 1974.

Hamilton, Edith. *Mythology*. New York and Toronto: New American Library, 1942.

Hardy, Thomas. *Tess of the D'Urbervilles*. New York and Toronto: New American Library, 1980.

Hemingway, Ernest. *A Farewell to Arms*. New York: Charles Scribner's Sons, 1957.

________. "Soldier's Home" in *In Our Time*. New York: Charles Scribner's Sons, 1958.

________. "The End of Something" in *In Our Time*. New York: Charles Scribner's Sons, 1958.

________. *The Sun Also Rises*. New York: Charles Scribner's Sons, 1954.

Hesse, Hermann. *Narcissus and Goldmund*. Trans. Ursule Molinaro. New York: Farrar, Straus and Giroux, 1968.

Huxley, Aldous, ed. *The Letters of D.H. Lawrence.* New York: The Viking Press, Inc., 1932.

Ibsen, Henrik. *Hedda Gabler.* Trans. Rolf Fjelde. In *Four Major Plays.* New York and Scarborough, Ontario: New American Library,1965.

________. *The Master Builder.* Trans. Rolf Fjelde. In *Four Major Plays.* New York and Scarborough, Ontario: New American Library, 1965.

Isherwood, Christopher. *The Berlin Stories.* New York: New Directions Publishing Corp., 1963.

James, Henry. *Partial Portraits.* Ann Arbor: The University of Michigan Press, 1970.

Janowsky, David S., Melitta Leff, and Richard S. Epstein. "Playing the Manic Game." In *Archives of General Psychiatry,* 22 (March, 1970), 252-261.

Keirsey, David. *Portraits of Temperament.* U.S.A.: Gnosology Books, Ltd., 1987.

Keirsey, David, and Marilyn Bates. *Please Understand Me: Character & Temperament Types.* U.S.A.: Gnosology Books, Ltd, 1984.

Lawrence, D.H. *The Fox* in *Four Short Novels of D.H. Lawrence.* New York: The Viking Press, Inc., 1972.

________. *Lady Chatterley's Lover.* New York: New American Library, 1959.

________. *Sons and Lovers.* New York: Penguin Books, 1981.

MacLeish, Archibald. *The Collected Poems of Archibald MacLeish.* Boston: Houghton Mifflin Company, 1962.

Nabokov, Vladimir. *Lolita.* New York: Greenwich House, 1982.

Scholes, Robert, Carl H. Klaus, and Michael Silverman. *Elements of Literature.* New York: Oxford University Press, 1978.

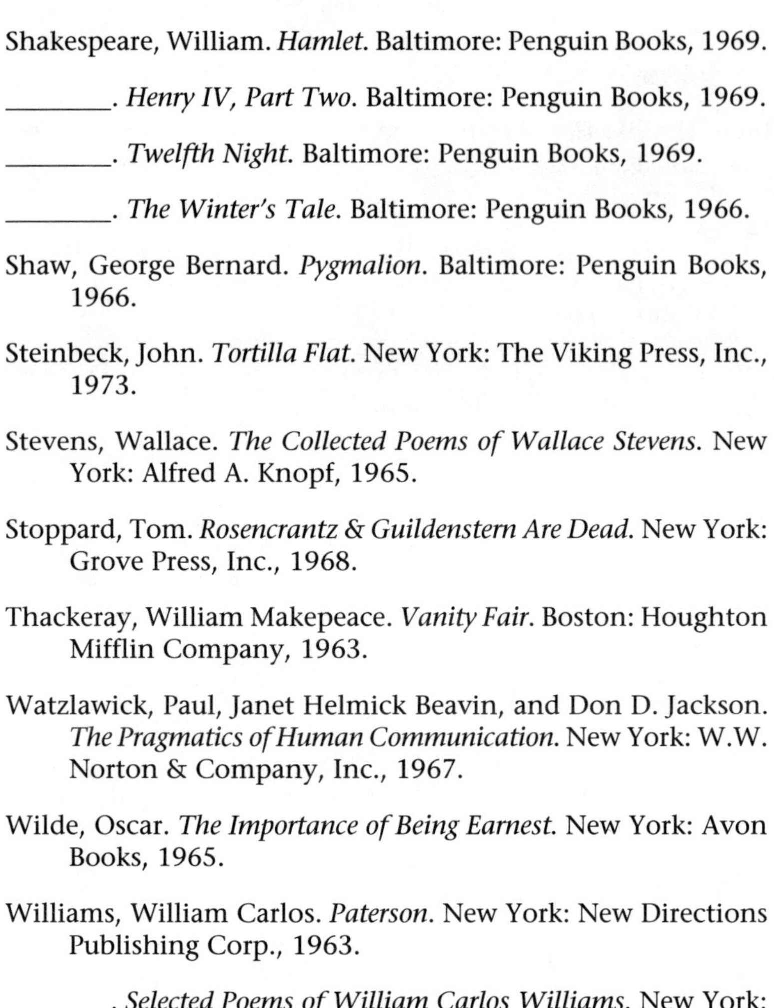

Shakespeare, William. *Hamlet.* Baltimore: Penguin Books, 1969.

________. *Henry IV, Part Two.* Baltimore: Penguin Books, 1969.

________. *Twelfth Night.* Baltimore: Penguin Books, 1969.

________. *The Winter's Tale.* Baltimore: Penguin Books, 1966.

Shaw, George Bernard. *Pygmalion.* Baltimore: Penguin Books, 1966.

Steinbeck, John. *Tortilla Flat.* New York: The Viking Press, Inc., 1973.

Stevens, Wallace. *The Collected Poems of Wallace Stevens.* New York: Alfred A. Knopf, 1965.

Stoppard, Tom. *Rosencrantz & Guildenstern Are Dead.* New York: Grove Press, Inc., 1968.

Thackeray, William Makepeace. *Vanity Fair.* Boston: Houghton Mifflin Company, 1963.

Watzlawick, Paul, Janet Helmick Beavin, and Don D. Jackson. *The Pragmatics of Human Communication.* New York: W.W. Norton & Company, Inc., 1967.

Wilde, Oscar. *The Importance of Being Earnest.* New York: Avon Books, 1965.

Williams, William Carlos. *Paterson.* New York: New Directions Publishing Corp., 1963.

________. *Selected Poems of William Carlos Williams.* New York: New Directions Publishing Corp., 1963.

Index

Page numbers in **boldface** reference a quotation.

Page numbers in *italics* reference a footnote.

Dr. Stephen Montgomery's *The Pygmalion Project: Love and Coercion Among the Types* is a four-volume explication of David Keirsey's theory of mating styles among the Artisan ("SP"), Guardian ("SJ"), Rational ("NT"), and Idealist ("NF") temperaments. Drawing on his experience in literature and temperament theory, Montgomery examines various kinds of Artisan characters and their Dionysian style of loving in this first volume. The series will continue with books (currently in progress) on the other three temperaments:

Volume 2: The Guardian will likely feature, among other relationships, Tess and Alec from Thomas Hardy's *Tess of the D'Urbervilles,* Nora and Torvald from Ibsen's *A Doll House,* and Katerina and Petruchio from Shakespeare's *The Taming of the Shrew.*

Volume 3: The Rational will likely include Elizabeth and Darcy from Jane Austen's *Pride and Prejudice,* John Galt and Dagny Taggart from Ayn Rand's *Atlas Shrugged,* and Henry Higgins and Eliza Doolittle from Bernard Shaw's *Pymaglion.*

Volume 4: The Idealist will likely include Cathy and Heathcliff from Emily Bronte's *Wuthering Heights,* Isabel Archer and Gilbert Osmond from Henry James's *The Portrait of a Lady,* and Paul and Miriam from D.H. Lawrence's *Sons and Lovers.*